Cultures of Creativity

Cultures of Creativity

The Centennial Exhibition of the Nobel Prize

REVISED EDITION

Ulf Larsson, Editor

Science History Publications/USA 2002

First published in Sweden in April, 2001 under the title:
Människor, miljöer och kreativitet: Nobelpriset 100 år

English language translation by Daniel M. Olson.

First published in the United States of America
by Science History Publications/USA
a division of Watson Publishing International
P.O. Box 493, Canton, MA 02021—0493

Nobel Museum Archives 2

Library of Congress Cataloging-in-Publication Data
Människor, miljöer och kreativitet. English.
    Cultures of creativity : the Centennial Exhibition of the Nobel prize /
Ulf Larsson, editor.—1st English language ed.
    p.   cm.   — (Nobel Museum Archives ; 2)
    Includes bibliographical references and index.
    ISBN 0-88135-288-8
    1. Nobel prizes—History.   2. Nobel prizes—Biography.   3. Nobel, Alfred Bernhard,
1833–1896. I. Larsson, Ulf, 1965-   . II. Title III. Series.
AS911.N9M34 2001
001.4'4—dc21   2001018355

Designed by Johan Cnattingius/Kingston AB.
Printed with financial support from:
Sven och Dagmar Saléns stiftelse and Konung Gustaf VI Adolfs fond för svensk kultur.
Printed by Åkessons Tryckeri, Emmaboda, Sweden, 2001.

Sponsors and contributors to the exhibition:
Cultures of Creativity: The Centennial Exhibition of the Nobel Prize

GLOBAL SPONSORS

ABB

Ericsson

Merrill Lynch

Skandia

Volvo

The rent for the exhibition hall in Stockholm is financed by the City of Stockholm.
The refurbishment of the exhibition space is performed with the support of Skanska
and AP Fastigheter.

CONTRIBUTORS

The Swedish Foundation for Strategic Research
The Bank of Sweden Tercentenary Foundation
The Swedish Foundation for International Cooperation in Research
    and Higher Education (STINT)
The Swedish Natural Science Research Council
The Swedish Medical Research Council
The Swedish Council for Planning and Coordination of Research
The Swedish Research Council for Engineering Sciences
The Swedish Council for Research in the Humanities and Social Sciences
The Swedish Business Development Agency (NUTEK)
The Wenner-Gren Foundations
The Torsten and Ragnar Söderbergs Foundations
The Jan Wallander and Tom Hedelius Foundation
The Swedish Council for Research in the Humanities and Social Sciences
The Carl Trygger Foundation for scientific research
The Vargöns Smelting Works Foundation
The Helge Axelsson Johnson Foundation
The Crafoord Foundation
The Royal Patriotic Society
The Magnus Bergvall Foundation

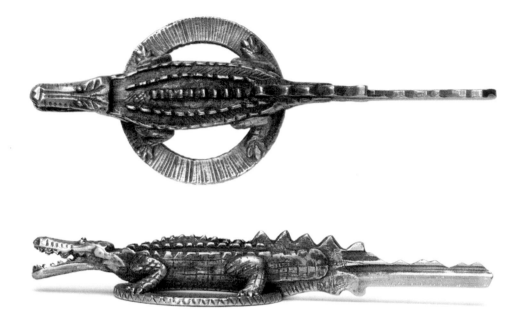

Russian physicist Piotr Kapitsa's key to the Mond laboratory in Cambridge, England, where he worked for a period during the 1920s and 1930s. The Crocodile shape has an explanation. "Crocodile" was Kapitsa's nick-name for his mentor Ernest Rutherford. Various explanations have been given for the nick-name. Late in life, Anna, Kapitsa's wife, said that none of the more fanciful suggestions were true. Nonetheless, one of Kapitsa's explanations is worth repeating:

"In Russia the crocodile is the symbol for the father of the family and is also regarded with awe and admiration because it has a stiff neck and cannot turn back. It just goes straight forward with gaping jaws—like science, like Rutherford."

Contents

Foreword

An Overview

The year 2001 marks the 100th anniversary of the Nobel Prizes, and during that span of time, more than 700 Nobel Prize laureates have been named. In 1997, the Nobel Foundation decided to celebrate this milestone with a centennial exhibition. While we await a permanent Nobel Museum in Stockholm, the exhibition will be shown partly in temporary facilities and partly as an international traveling exhibition. But given limited space, how could we present the stories of the lives of these more than 700 fascinating people and their important contributions? Such an ambitious exhibition would risk either becoming ponderously overloaded, or (perhaps even worse) superficial. No, it would not be possible to show everything in this, the first exhibition produced by the as yet homeless Nobel Museum.

A selection of laureates should not be limited to the most famous, however; such an exhibition would have been quite predictable ("Einstein & Co."). We needed to find a criterion for the choice, a general concept, that could be adapted to prize recipients in the natural sciences as well as those in peace and literature. We also needed to find a theme that would be of interest in and of itself, apart from the centennial celebration of the prizes.

The Nobel Foundation decided to focus the Centennial Exhibition on the concept of creativity. In viewing the Nobel Prizes over one hundred years, the exhibition seeks to answer the question "What is creativity, and how can it best be promoted?" This question is always a current one, and the history of the Nobel Prizes offers a unique basis for comparisons of the creativity of scientists, authors, and promoters of peace. Interest in creativity as reflected in literature, research, and general debate centers around two poles: the individuals and their environment. There is therefore, also, a tension or dichotomy built into the exhibition. It invites the public to ponder the question, "What is most meaningful in the creative process: the creativity of the individuals or the environments in which their work is carried out?"

To highlight these questions, a selection was made of about thirty Nobel Prize recipients and about ten "creative milieus," that is, places which have generated a remarkably large number of Nobel Prizes during the 1900s. The centennial exhibition serves as a background against which questions about creativity and creative environments can be discussed. The exhibition provides no definitive answers, but instead offers "food for thought." It is our hope that visitors will find the exhibition both stimulating and thought-provoking.

This is not to say, however, that creativity is the only interesting aspect of the contributions of Nobel Laureates. It is only one perspective from which we may view the many-faceted history of the Nobel Prizes. In the future, the Nobel Museum intends to produce new exhibitions featuring different themes, which will cast these captivating stories in other lights.

The Nobel Museum has the potential to become the much sought after bridge between the "two cultures," between the sciences and the humanities; a new type of science center that places scientific development in its cultural and social context. This exhibition, "Cultures of Creativity: The Centennial Exhibition of the Nobel Prize," is the first step toward this goal.

Svante Lindqvist, Director
The Nobel Museum
Stockholm, December 10, 2000

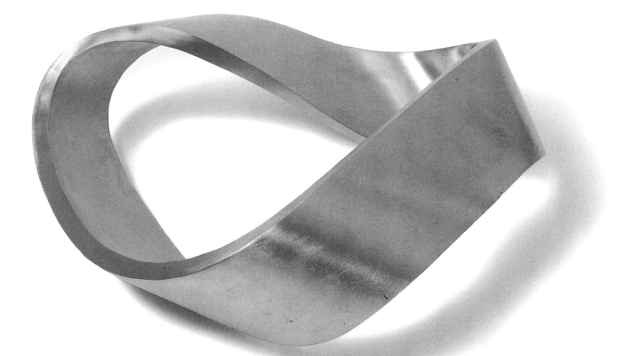

The Möbius strip has only one surface, though we experience that it has two. Wole Soyinka writes that the Möbius strip "is a very simple figure of aesthetic and scientific truths and contradictions. In this sense, it is the symbol of Ogun in particular, and an evolution from the self-devouring snake which he sometimes hangs around his neck and which symbolizes the doom of repetition." A section of Soyinka's poem "Idanre" reads:

Evolution of the self-devouring snake to spatials
New in symbol, banked loop of the 'Mobius strip'
And interlock of re-creative rings, one surface
Yet full comb of angles, uni-plane, yet sensuous with
Complexities of mind and motion.

Introduction

In his speech at the banquet following the 1986 Nobel Prize awards ceremony, Wole Soyinka, recipient of the prize in literature, made a surprising statement. He claimed that Alfred Nobel's actual predecessor was to be found not in the cold Nordic countries, but rather in Soyinka's own African culture, in Ogun, the god of Yoruban mythology. As with all good dinner speeches, this bit of humor also carried a serious message.

Ogun is the Yoruban god of creativity. Yoruban mythology divides the world into three realms: the world of ancestors, the world of the living, and the world of the unborn. There is yet another level: the realm of constant change. Here the cosmic will is given expression and reality takes form. Ogun dared to look into this realm, and with knowledge, art, visionary thinking and the mystic creativity of science, crossed over into it. Ogun symbolizes the desire and instinct of creativity, creativity's essence.

The concept of creativity has deep associations with Alfred Nobel; not only with Nobel's own work as an inventor, but also with his thinking and his desire to reward creativity. Creativity is also something which unites all Nobel Prize recipients. Each of them has been rewarded for having done something innovative.

But they have reached their creative achievements in many different ways. Creativity is many-faceted and difficult to capture. On a basic level, creativity may not seem so complicated—an ability to break away from established patterns and create something new. But then the picture becomes more difficult to grasp. How is creativity achieved? Through wild rebellion against the establishment? A quiet walk away from the well-trodden paths? The inspiration for some revolutionary advances seems to appear from nowhere, while in other cases only a hard-fought battle will turn the status quo upside-down. Creativity is sometimes the fruit of consequential, goal-oriented work, but at other times coincidence seems to be the source of a groundbreaking discovery. Not even the very heart of creativity—the ability to break away from convention—is entirely unclouded: creativity may build upon previous discoveries and traditions even though it brings innovative combinations and unions.

In the creative process there is tension between the inner workings of the individual's mind and the stimulation and effects of the individual's surroundings. Creativity may be peaceful work performed in quiet solitude—yet it may also be dependent upon a rushing flood of input from the surrounding world.

Some of the many facets of creativity show themselves even in the life and work of Alfred Nobel. Nobel worked together with others, but he also longed for the solitude of his office or laboratory. He was an imaginative dreamer, but also a rational technician and a polished and serious entrepreneur. He loved work, and found happiness in his thriving enterprises, yet he grew weary of administrative concerns and never ending legal proceedings.

Nor is creativity entirely positive and good. If we return to Yoruban mythology for a moment, we see that Ogun, the god of creativity, shows a basic duality in this respect. Along with creativity follows its "complementary" aspect—destruction. Thus Ogun is the god of both creativity and war.

Traces painting by Gao Xingjian, Nobel Laureate in literature 2000.

The light and the dark sides of creativity were obvious in Alfred Nobel's inventions, which could be used not only to create a better world, but also to destroy it. Nobel was painfully aware of this fact, and was often plagued by it. In her memoirs, Bertha von Suttner writes that the first time they met, Nobel told her "I should like to invent a substance or a machine of such terrible destruction that it would make war forever impossible."

Even the discoveries of many Nobel laureates have shown themselves to be two-sided. Some have been used for purposes less than good, and others have had unforeseen consequences. Creativity may be driven by sometimes opposing forces and conditions. There may be a will to serve the greater good without regard for personal profit. But there may also be a desire for glory. There is more to milieus which foster creativity than pleasant intellectual stimulation. There is also disagreement and fierce competition. Creative people are often possessed by their creativity. It becomes a need which must be satisfied, sometimes to the point of reducing their existence

outside work to suffering. While we cannot ignore the darker sides of creativity, our faith is that creativity is among the best aspects of human existence. Creativity frees humanity from destructive desperation and gives hope.

The Centennial Exhibition of the Nobel Prize seeks to explore the variety of creativity. This is also the ambition of this book, produced in conjunction with the exhibition. Rather than explain the achievements of Nobel Laureates in science, literature and peace work, we have chosen to illuminate various phases in the creative processes which led up to those achievements. Specifically, the focus is upon the tension in their creative work between inner processes and outer circumstances. The Nobel Prizes provide an opportunity to show the parallels between creative activity in the various prize areas.

This book is neither strictly an exhibition catalog nor a free-standing collection of texts. The initial choices of subject matter to be presented were made by working groups in 1998–1999. The material produced at that time

Niels Bohr and Albert Einstein, two of the pioneers in 20th century physics, were often on different tracks in their interpretation of the new physics. However, that did not prevent a creative exchange of thoughts.

became the basis for the exhibition as well as this book. Naturally, the material has been given different expressions in these different media. The exhibition consists mainly of moving film images in combination with artifacts. The book makes use of photographs of the artifacts as well as additional photographs not shown in the exhibition. The book allows the text greater space and another format than the displays and film manuscripts of the museum exhibit. During the years they are on display, both the permanent version of the exhibit in Stockholm as well as the international touring version will be renewed and changed, such that the book will not always reflect the exact contents of the exhibition.

However, the general outline of the book does agree with that of the exhibition. The first section, "Alfred Nobel and His Times," covers the ideas and circumstances underlying Alfred Nobel's will, in which he provided for the establishment of the Nobel Prizes. The second section, "The Nobel System," tells how Nobel's wishes were made reality: how the Nobel Foundation was established, how the prize awards are celebrated, as well as how the prizes have been interpreted. "Individual Creativity," the third section, presents the creative efforts of a number of Nobel Laureates—the driving forces behind their work, the creative processes they have undergone, or the achievements they have made. The fourth section, "Creative milieus," presents a number of milieus which have been significant for the creative development of Nobel Laureates, and explores how an environment can stimulate creative achievement and how fruitful exchange of ideas and experiences can be encouraged. The main theme of the exhibition—the tension between individual creativity and the environments where the creation takes place—is reflected in the third and fourth sections, which are also the most comprehensive.

The Centennial Exhibition of the Nobel Prize celebrates creativity. Like Wole Soyinka in his speech at the Nobel Banquet in 1986, we share Alfred Nobel's hope that humanity's capacity for change and creativity may lead to something good.

The section of Alfred Nobel's will where he established the Nobel Prizes reads:

"The whole of my remaining realizable estate shall be dealt with in the following way: the capital, invested in safe securities by my executors, shall constitute a fund, the interest on which shall be annually distributed in the form of prizes to those who, during the preceding year, shall have conferred the greatest benefit on mankind. The said interest shall be divided into five equal parts, which shall be apportioned as follows: one part to the person who shall have made the most important discovery or invention within the field of physics; one part to the person who shall have made the most important chemical discovery or improvement; one part to the person who shall have made the most important discovery within the domain of physiology or medicine; one part to the person who shall have produced in the field of literature the most outstanding work of an idealistic tendency; and one part to the person who shall have done the most or the best work for fraternity between nations, for the abolition or reduction of standing armies and for the holding and promotion of peace congresses. The prizes for physics and chemistry shall be awarded by the Swedish Academy of Sciences; that for physiology or medical works by the Karolinska Institute in Stockholm; that for literature by the Academy in Stockholm; and that for champions of peace by a committee of five persons to be elected by the Norwegian Storting. It is my express wish that in awarding the prizes no consideration be given to the nationality of the candidates, but that the most worthy shall receive the prize, whether he be Scandinavian or not."

Alfred Nobel and His Times

On November 27, 1895, Alfred Nobel put his signature to what would become one of the most famous last wills in the world. This will was not based on last-minute emotion. It had been preceded by several earlier versions, and the road leading up to the final draft wound its way through the intellectual and material landscapes of the day. The will was the sum of Alfred Nobel himself, people he had met, places where he had spent time, and the thoughts that had confronted him.

One reason his will came into being at all was that Alfred Nobel was childless. Who would inherit the huge fortune he had made through his inventions and industries? Some of his relatives received part of the inheritance, as did a few other individuals. But Nobel had other plans for the largest portion of his wealth: it would be managed in a fund, and the interest used to reward and support people with good ideas.

Alfred Nobel's will was an affirmation of belief in human creativity, a belief prevalent in his day. The will mirrors common views of the late 1800s regarding creativity, progress, and development. But Alfred Nobel was a unique individual and, in a number of ways, his will is an expression of his personality.

What were the ideas behind Alfred Nobel's will? Why were individuals to be rewarded? Why were the prizes to be awarded internationally? And why were the prizes to be given specifically in the areas of physics, chemistry, medicine, literature, and peace?

Alfred Nobel. Oil painting by Emil Österman painted after Nobel's death.

Alfred Nobel was born at Norrlandsgatan in Stockholm.

Alfred Nobel's younger brother Emil was killed in an accident in
the laboratory at Heleneborg in Stockholm on September 3, 1864.

Alfred Nobel around 20 years of age.

Alfred Nobel at the bridge in Dolce Aqua, Taggia.

Alfred Nobel in a park in San Remo.

Björkborn in Bofors was Alfred Nobel's last home in Sweden.

Alfred Nobel and Wilhelm Unge
outside the Villa Nobel in San Remo.

Alfred Nobel the Man

"Engineer, medium height, brown hair, oval face, healthy skin and blue eyes."

This description of Alfred Nobel was entered into the passport registry of the Stockholm Police in 1863. Who was this engineer of medium height? Was he a genius and a success? Spiritual and worldly wise? Friendly and kind? Sickly and in poor spirits? Lonely and unhappy?

Alfred Nobel's own description of himself was not particularly complimentary: "a worthless instrument of cogitation, alone in the world and with thoughts heavier than anyone can imagine." In a letter to his brother Ludvig Nobel in 1887, he wrote: "Alfred Nobel—pathetic, half alive, should have been strangled by a humanitarian doctor when he made his screeching entrance into the world. *Greatest merits:* Keeps his neck clean and is never a burden to anyone. *Greatest fault:* Lacks family, cheerful spirits, and strong stomach. *Greatest and only petition:* Not to be buried alive. *Greatest sin:* Does not worship Mammon. *Important events in his life:* None."

Yet other descriptions of Alfred Nobel reveal a pleasant and fascinating person who enjoyed the company of others. His life seems rich and varied, despite his many disappointments.

Nobel was born in 1833. He had many brothers and sisters, but only he and his brothers Robert and Ludvig survived to adulthood. His father and brothers devoted themselves to inventions and industrial activity, as did young Alfred. Much of his life would revolve around his work with all its attendant joys and sorrows. His experiments certainly made him happy, but a difficult blow was dealt him when his younger brother Emil died in an accident connected to one of his experiments. In addition to his industrial successes, he also experienced many setbacks in business and in legal proceedings. His emotional life was not especially harmonious, and his romances were for the most part unhappy.

Alfred Nobel was a reticent man, and he took no delight in titles and awards. In his letters, he wrote that he wished "all manifestations to go to blazes," and begged "to be preserved from medals and other such tin plating."

Why did Nobel want to reward individuals with prizes? Popular thinking of the day held that progress was driven forward by ingenious and industrious individuals. It was thought that such persons were often held back by circumstances beyond their control, and if these impediments could be removed, development would be promoted. In his day, Alfred Nobel was one of the richest men in Europe. Yet he had also experienced much adversity in his work. Perhaps looking back over his own life gave him the desire to give people with good ideas the economic means to realize them.

Alfred Nobel's suitcase. Nobel spent a lot of time traveling and carried with him cutlery as well as writing materials.

The winter garden at Alfred Nobel's home at Avenue Malakoff in Paris, where he moved in 1873. Culturally, the city was the capital of Europe—a meeting place for a multitude of artists, writers and other intellectuals from all over world. "Here every mongrel smells of civilization," Alfred Nobel wrote with delight.

Cosmopolitan

When Alfred Nobel was only nine years old, his family moved from Stockholm to St. Petersburg, Russia. When he was 17 years old, he set off on his first study trip to Europe and North America. His life would always have an international flavor. At the end of his life, when he once again purchased a home in Sweden, he already had three luxurious houses, in Ardeer, Scotland, in Paris and in San Remo, Italy. His relatives also lived in various countries. His brothers Robert and Ludvig lived in Baku in present-day Azerbaijan, where they had established an oil industry.

Alfred Nobel's life was extremely mobile, yet also typical of his times. Industrial developments placed great demands on systems of transportation for both people and products. Sea and land communications were developing quickly. While travel was more rapid than ever before, it still often took days, weeks, and months to go from one place to another.

Construction of the railways of Europe led to great demand for Nobel's explosives. And yet, his far-reaching business empire would not have been possible without the new communications networks. In the year 1873, Alfred Nobel had no fewer than 16 dynamite factories in 14 countries. At his death in 1896, there were Nobel companies in 20 countries, with a total of 93 factories. Strict security laws concerning explosives had forced him to build "a factory in every country." In order to watch over his interests and to keep ahead of his competitors, Nobel traveled from factory to factory. Even though these were the days of the telegraph, he felt that his business affairs required his personal presence. To keep his empire intact, he had to travel. He had no agents or secretary, only the respective managers at the various factories. Nobel spent a great portion of his life on trains and boats, accompanied by his suitcase and briefcase.

Alfred Nobel was a citizen of the world, well oriented in the languages of many countries and cultures. His cosmopolitan existence explains why the Nobel prizes are awarded without regard to nationality. In his will he wrote: "It is my express wish that in awarding the prizes no consideration be given to the nationality of the candidates, but that the most worthy shall receive the prize, whether he be Scandinavian or not."

Alfred Nobel's laboratory in San Remo.

A small laminating roller and gas heater
from Alfred Nobel's laboratory.

Instruments from the laboratory of Alfred Nobel. At the center is a branch with a valve. At the right is a heating and drying apparatus with a rotating pulley. The glass items are for distilling.

Inventor and Progressive

"If I have a thousand ideas a year, and only one turns out to be good, I'm satisfied."

Alfred Nobel had a myriad of ideas. Many of them led to poor results, but a few were incredibly significant. Nobel fits rather well the stereotypical image of the ingenious inventor, an important person in the nineteenth century. The transforming power of science and technology was apparent in the world Alfred Nobel lived in, and its possibilities were acknowledged to a great extent. By mastering, controlling, conquering, and triumphing over nature, mankind would create its own future. This optimism about the possibilities of technology, together with a constant flow of capital and ideas across national boundaries were important for the industrialization of the 1800s. Technological optimism was also an important background to the ideas and life work of Alfred Nobel.

Nobel was born to invention. His father Immanuel was an inventor, and Alfred himself became interested in science and technology, especially chemistry. Eventually his attention turned to the liquid explosive known as nitroglycerine. Together with his father, he tried to tame nitroglycerine and make it a reliable explosive. The most famous result of his many years of work was dynamite. By allowing nitroglycerine to be absorbed by kieselguhr, an easily handled and moldable explosive was obtained. The developments leading up to dynamite had produced a number of other important inventions. Nobel's development of the detonator was equally as epoch-making as dynamite. Other important inventions were blasting gelatine, in which a combination of gun cotton and nitroglycerine were united into a powerful but reliable explosive, and ballastite, or smokeless powder.

Alfred Nobel had more than 300 of his patents approved. While most of his inventions were related to the development of explosives, he was also interested in artificial silk, hot air engines, gas meters, artificial leather, aluminum boats, and more. Most of his inventions yielded no economic profit, but dynamite made him rich.

Alfred Nobel was an inventor, a researcher, and a businessman. What drove him? Profit? The good of human-

One of the industrial projects Alfred Nobel was involved in was the so-called Svea bicycle developed by the Ljungström brothers. It was designed so that the pedals moved in an up-and-down motion instead of rotating.

Patent certificate for one of Alfred Nobel's inventions.

ity? The creative stimulus of invention? Presumably it was a combination of all of these. When he ran into difficulties in business, Nobel longed for his laboratory. In one letter he wrote:

"I am sick of the explosives trade, wherein one continually stumbles over accidents, restrictive regulations, red tape, pedants, knavery, and other nuisances. I long for quiet and wish to devote my time to scientific research, which is impossible when every day brings new worry."

Alfred Nobel was also an industrial leader. His life spanned the transition period between pre-industrial society and the modern socialized state. Some employers took great responsibility for the welfare of their workers; others maintained that society should take this responsibility or that the workers should organize their own aid associations. It is not entirely clear what Alfred Nobel's views were, but he was engaged in social issues and his factories offered health care, insurance, and old-age pensions for their employees. Nobel described himself as "a kind of social democrat, but with modifications." He had a strong belief in the rights and potential of the individ-

ual. It might be more correct to describe him as a liberal with social interests.

How did Nobel view technological developments? He was hardly of an optimistic nature, and was quite pessimistic regarding the world situation. However, he probably had some belief in the potential of development, and he took a bright view of the possibilities of science. His will can be interpreted as an expression of this belief.

Physics and chemistry were Nobel's own areas of scientific specialization. It was natural that he named them first when he indicated the disciplines he wanted to establish prizes for. The prizes in physiology and medicine can be seen as an expression for his belief in the potential of science to create a world free from sickness.

Perhaps the will also gives expression to a certain view of creative activity in science and technology. Apparently discoveries and inventions were emphasized rather than deep, methodical scientific work. Alfred Nobel's own work as an inventor is evident in his choice of words such as "invention," "discovery," and "improvement" rather than "work," "achievement," or "research."

Dynamite and fuse. Dynamite became the most successful of Alfred Nobel's inventions.

The manufacture of explosives involved risk. In 1874 an accident occurred in Nobel's factory at Vinterviken in Stockholm.

Books from Alfred Nobel's library.

The Idealist

Alfred Nobel's desire to reward those who "shall have conferred the greatest benefit on mankind" is clearly idealistic in nature. While Nobel's idealism was evident in all of the prizes, it was at its most obvious in the Literature and Peace prizes.

"A recluse without books and ink is already while living a dead man."

Although Alfred Nobel was most at home with his work and inventions, literature and writing became his second home. As late as 35 years of age, he considered "taking to the pen to earn my daily bread." Among the papers he left after his death were his attempts at writing—a handful of early poems, a few drafts of several discourse novels, and a tragedy.

During his youth in St. Petersburg, Nobel came into contact with the Russian writers Pushkin and Turgenjev, as well as the English Romantics Wordsworth, Shelley,

and his favorite poet, Lord Byron. At his death, Nobel had a library of just over 1,500 volumes. For the most part it consisted of popular fiction in the original languages, but also classics and works by philosophers, theologians, historians, and other scientists.

The collection contained many classics: Musset, Tegnér, Shakespeare, Scott, Goethe, Schiller—all authors whom Nobel enjoyed reading and loved to quote. He also read contemporary literature such as Hugo, Maupassant, Tolstoy, Ibsen, and Strindberg. He appreciated the modern literary currents, but felt that naturalism sometimes went too far. He was more easily charmed by writers inclined to idealism. Toward the end of his life Nobel became more interested in philosophy. His own ideas were anchored in the Enlightenment tradition and were influenced by the contemporary movements of positivism and Darwinism.

Nobel's will gives witness to his lifelong love of literature—one of the prizes was to be presented to "the person

Alfred Nobel's copy of Bertha von Suttner's book *Die Waffen nieder.*

Bertha von Suttner.

who shall have produced in the field of literature the most outstanding work in an ideal direction."

In the late 1800s, the peace movement was yet another expression of belief in social projects on a grand scale to improve the world. During the later part of his life, Alfred Nobel became involved in the peace movement to a degree. This may seem paradoxical; several of his inventions had military uses, and he had undeniable interests in the arms industry.

Nobel's engagement in the cause of peace also had a personal background. In 1876, Nobel employed Austrian Bertha von Kinsky as his secretary. She worked for Nobel in Paris for only a short time before traveling back to Austria to get married. Bertha von Suttner, as she was known after her marriage, and Alfred Nobel nonetheless kept in contact by letter for the rest of his life. Among other things, they shared an interest in literature.

Bertha von Suttner became an international figure in the peace movement thanks to her powerful book *Die Waffen nieder*, which was published in many languages and in numerous editions. Although Nobel had shown some earlier interest in the cause of world peace, Von Suttner encouraged his involvement.

His attitude toward the possibilities of the peace movement seems to have been somewhat ambivalent. According to Bertha von Suttner, he said that his factories might perhaps show themselves to have more power than her peace congresses:

"For in the day that two armies are capable of destroying each other in a second, all civilized nations will surely recoil before a war and dismiss their troops."

Nobel maintained that the peace movement was based on a partly unrealistic program, although he did believe that an international court might have some power.

What is likely is that his contact with Bertha von Suttner was a contributing factor to Alfred Nobel's establishment of a peace prize. In 1905, von Suttner herself was the recipient of the Nobel Peace Prize.

The Nobel System

On December 10, 1896, Alfred Nobel died in San Remo. On December 30 of the same year his will was opened in Stockholm. Its basic intention was clear. The major part of his enormous fortune was to be placed in a fund so that prizes within five specified fields could be awarded annually. It is not surprising that this caused a certain consternation and disappointment among his relatives; it also caused controversy in wider circles.

Many Swedes were upset, thinking that the prizes should only be awarded to Swedes. Some suggested that Alfred Nobel had not acted as a patriot. But others thought the prizes would give Sweden the reputation of being a nation of culture.

The will was rather brief and provided no details about how Nobel's ideas should be realized. The lack of formal legal language in the will even caused its validity to be questioned. A number of other question were raised. Would his relatives accept the will? Would the institutions that had been chosen to award the prizes accept their assignments? How would the assets be transformed into money and gathered into a fund? Who would administer this fund? And, if the prizes were eventually established, how would the prize winners be selected?

After four years of discussions and investigations, a solution was reached. The outcome was the establishment of a system of institutions, committees, and regulations for the adminstration of the fund and the determination of how the prize winners should be selected and rewarded.

Barbara McClintock, laureate in physiology or medicine in 1983.

The Nobel Prizes became a reality. What meaning have they acquired? How did they become the most prestigious awards in science, literature, and peace work? What do they stand for in the public's opinion?

< Tun Channareth accepts the Nobel Peace Prize at Oslo City Hall in 1997. Tun Channareth accepted the prize as a representative of the International Campaign to Ban Landmines.

Alfred Nobels testamente.

Storartad välmening — stor artade missgrepp.

I lördags afton bragte *N. D. A.* te stamentets ordalydelse; *A. B.,* som mai kan förstå redan förut känt donsamma

When Alfred Nobel's will was made public, different views were expressed in the Swedish press. The ambivalence is expressed in the headline "Grand intentions–grand mistakes."

Ragnar Sohlman made the greatest efforts to make the Nobel Prizes a reality. As a young engineer he was the assistant of Alfred Nobel and from 1929 to 1946 he was the executive director of the Nobel Foundation.

Creating a framework for the realization of Alfred Nobel's wishes was a huge and diicult undertaking. It was largely due to the work of Nobel's young assistant Ragnar Sohlman that the Nobel Prizes came into being at all. In his last will and testament, Nobel had appointed Sohlman as one of those who were to fulfill his intentions. Sohlman and Nobel's legal advisor Carl Lindhagen and their colleagues displayed great care, skill and patience in carrying out this duty.

The question arose immediately as to where the legal proceedings should take place. Deciding just where the cosmopolitan Nobel's home was proved to be no easy task. In the end, the proceedings were undertaken in the county court at Karlskoga, Sweden, since Nobel's last home in Sweden was at Björkborn, just outside Karlskoga.

One task for Sohlman and his colleagues was to see to it that the different assets Alfred Nobel had in various places around the world were transferred to Sweden. Would the countries in which the funds were located demand taxes and legal fees? In some countries, retrieving the assets was quite easy. In others, it was difficult. To avoid bringing unwanted attention to his activities, Ragnar Sohlman personally transported various assets between the bank and diplomatic agencies. He rode through Paris in a horse and carriage, sitting on a chest

full of financial papers, which he guarded with a pistol.

Alfred Nobel's relatives took a doubtful view of the will. Not only were they disappointed that they would not inherit the entire fortune, but transferring the fortune into secure financial papers posed a special problem for the branch of the family that operated the Nobel oil industry in Baku. Alfred Nobel's shares in the company were so large that liquidating them would probably have caused the value of the stocks to plummet. His shares also "tipped the scales," and the family risked losing control of the company if the shares were sold. After some negotiations, an agreement was reached. The branch of the Nobel family living in Russia abstained from contesting the will. The fact that Nobel's nephew Emanuel Nobel did not want to act against his paternal uncle's will was of great importance to the establishment of the Nobel Prizes.

In his will, Nobel indicated the institutions that were to select the recipients of the prizes: for the prize in physics and chemistry, the Royal Swedish Academy of Sciences; for the prize in physiology or medicine, the Karolinska Institute; for the prize in literature, the Swedish Academy; and for the peace prize, a special committee appointed by the *Storting*, the Parliament of Norway. There was in fact some uncertainty concerning the Swedish Academy. The will names "the Academy in

The first ledger of the Nobel Foundation. One of the main tasks of the Nobel Foundation is to administer the fund that generates the prize money.

Stockholm," which after consideration was interpreted as the Swedish Academy, although it was not entirely certain that this was the Academy that Nobel had meant.

Nor was it at all certain that the institutions would accept this huge responsibility. Some members of the institutions felt that the task lay outside the activities that the institutions had pursued until then, and would distort their work. The point was also made that members of these institutions might be subject to temptations that would corrupt them. However, after long discussions, each of the institutions accepted the responsibility. Certainly, one reason that they could accept this task was that they were promised increased resources for the purpose of researching and judging possible prize recipients. Among other things, they were also given the right to establish so-called Nobel Institutes for research in their respective prize areas.

In Sweden, the arrangements regarding the Peace Prize were regarded as especially problematic. That the prize was to be awarded by a committee appointed by the Norwegian Storting was especially sensitive, since Sweden and Norway were in a political union at the time. Nobel's seeming unwillingness to entrust a Swedish institution with this task was interpreted by some as an insult. It was felt that this would injure Sweden's interests and complicate relations between the two countries. Still others felt that it was generally unwise to give such a responsibility to a committee appointed by a political body.

Reaching a suitable form of administration for Nobel's fortune was another task for those carrying out the will. What was meant by "fund" was not entirely clear. Some of Nobel's relatives felt that they should be responsible for administering the fund. However, the result of the legal proceedings was that a foundation—the Nobel Foundation—was established instead. It was decided that the Nobel Foundation would be overseen by a Board of Directors who in turn would be chosen by the members of the prize-awarding institutions.

The monetary amount of the Nobel Prizes depends upon how well the Nobel Foundation has succeeded in administering its capital during the year. The size of the Nobel fortune and its yield have varied over time. Alfred Nobel's will stated that the endowment was to be placed in "safe securities." As a result, the annual yield was rather low for many years. During the economically turbulent period between the two world wars, the endowment came close to being exhausted. In the 1950s the Foundation's statutes were changed so that its capital could be invested in stocks. Initially, the Nobel Foundation was rather heavily taxed, but has been tax free since 1946. However, it was not until the 1990s that the monetary value of the Prizes again reached the levels they were at in the earliest years.

Diploma for the Nobel Prize in literature of 1931 which was awarded for the poetry of Erik Axel Karlfeldt. Karlfeldt had died a few months before the prize was awarded.

Alfred Nobel's will provided no further details about the arrangement of the decision-making process. To guarantee a thorough examination of the qualifications of potential candidates, a comprehensive procedure for the award decisions was outlined in the statutes of the Foundation. Certain differences exist between the procedures for the various prizes, but in general they are the same.

For each Prize there is a special Nobel Committee. In the case of the Peace Prize, the Nobel Committee makes the decision regarding the prize. For the other prizes, the Committee's duty is to carry out preparations and provide advice for the decision-making process. Each committee has three to five members appointed by the respective prize-awarding institution.

The basis for the committees' work is the review of the nominations. The statutes of the prize-awarding institutions designate the persons who have the right to nominate. Along with others, all previous prize recipients have the right to make nominations. In September, the Committees send out letters calling for nominations. Anyone who nominates him- or herself is disqualified. Nominations must be received no later than January 31 of the following year, when a comprehensive study of the nominations begins. An initial examination usually narrows the nominations to a smaller number of candidates. For advice in the decision-making process, the Committee

has the right to call upon outside, independent experts. In October the decisions are made. In any given year, up to three persons may share a Nobel Prize in a particular discipline. The Peace Prize is the only prize that is sometimes awarded to institutions instead of individuals.

The procedure is shrouded in secrecy. The statutes state that divergent opinions may not be recorded in the protocol. Reports and discussions surrounding the decision are secret, but the documents become available for research purposes after 50 years.

Alfred Nobel's will provides no directions for how the prizes are to be presented. It was decided that December 10, the date of Alfred Nobel's death, would be the day on which Nobel laureates would receive their awards.

The prizes are signified by the awarding of a medal and a diploma. The presentation of the Peace Prize takes place in Oslo, and all other prizes are awarded in Stockholm. It was decided that the awards should be made with a certain degree of ceremony. At the award ceremony in Stockholm, the prizes are presented by the King of Sweden. The award ceremony is followed by a banquet. In the beginning, the Nobel festivities were not large affairs, but today they have grown into a grand gala. The visit of the Nobel laureates to Stockholm also brings additional events other than the award ceremonies. Among other things, each Nobel laureate presents a lecture.

The front side of all the Nobel Medals features a portrait of Alfred Nobel, but the back sides vary. The medal of the Royal Swedish Academy of Sciences—for the prizes in physics and chemistry—represents Nature in the form of a goddess resembling Isis, emerging from the clouds and holding in her arms a cornucopia. The veil that covers her cold and austere face is held by the Genius of Science. The medal of the Karolinska Institute—for the prize in physiology or medicine—represents the Genius of Medicine holding an open book in her lap, gathering in a bowl the water welling out from a rock in order to allay a sick girl's thirst. The medal of the Swedish Academy—for the prize in literature—represents a young man sitting under a laurel tree who, enchanted, listens to and writes down the song of the Muse. The medal of the Norwegian Nobel Committee—for the peace prize—represents a group of three men forming a fraternal bond.

The Swedish medals bear the Latin inscription "Inventas vitam juvat excoluisse per artes," which is taken from Virgil's *Aeneid* and means "And they who bettered life on earth by new-found mastery." The Norwegian medal has the inscription "Pro pace et fraternitatet gentium," which means "For peace and fraternization between the peoples." The Swedish medals are designed by Erik Lindberg and the Norwegian by Gustav Vigeland.

The medal for The Bank of Sweden Prize in Economic Sciences in Memory of Alfred Nobel has a picture of Alfred Nobel on its front side and the symbol of the Royal Swedish Academy of Sciences on the back side. The medal was designed by Gunvor Svensson-Lundkvist.

The Nobel Prize ceremony in the Stockholm Concert Hall in 1995.

Literature laureate Isaac Bashevis Singer reading the translations of the speeches at the Nobel Ceremony in 1978. The oral presentations at the Nobel Ceremony are in Swedish.

Nelly Sachs accepts the Nobel Prize in Literature 1966.

The Nobel Laureates of 1971 with their medals and diplomas: Simon Kuznets, Pablo Neruda, Earl Sutherland, Gerhard Herzberg, and Dennis Gabor.

Abdus Salam, Nobel Laureate in physics 1979, shows his diploma to his family.

The Nobel Banquet in Stockholm City Hall in 1996.

Swedish Princess Christina and Isaac Bashevis Singer at the Nobel Banquet 1978.

Medicine laureate Niels Jerne and Swedish Queen Silvia at the Nobel Banquet in 1984.

Medicine laureate Francis Crick dancing at the Nobel Banquet in 1962.

At the beginning of the 20th century the Swedish Academy was harshly criticized. The radicals in Swedish culture saw the academy and its permanent secretary Carl David af Wirsén as antiquated and conservative. The criticism was seen prominently in the comic journals. The decision to award the first Nobel Prize in literature to the French poet Sully Prudhomme was seen as an expression of the old-fashioned ideals of the academy. Many critics thought the prize should have been awarded to the great Russian writer Leo Tolstoy. One of these critics was Sweden's own great writer August Strindberg.

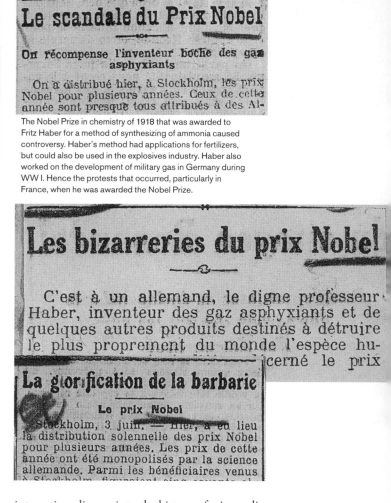

The Nobel Prize in chemistry of 1918 that was awarded to Fritz Haber for a method of synthesizing of ammonia caused controversy. Haber's method had applications for fertilizers, but could also be used in the explosives industry. Haber also worked on the development of military gas in Germany during WW I. Hence the protests that occurred, particularly in France, when he was awarded the Nobel Prize.

The Nobel Prizes have come to be one of the most prestigious honors in the world, for several reasons. Certainly one distinction of the Nobel Prizes is that their monetary amounts have been so large. Yet the size of the awards is probably not the foremost explanation for the high regard in which the prizes are held. That the Nobel Prizes were the first international awards of their kind certainly contributed to their prestige from the beginning. The fact that the first prizes were awarded to researchers who were recognized and known gave the science prizes a favorable image from the start. The nomination procedure and its thorough evaluations also lent credibility. And perhaps Sweden and Norway's position as small, not especially politically powerful countries in an isolated corner of the world has contributed to a reputation for impartiality.

Nonetheless, the decision as to who receives a Nobel Prize is still the result of human judgments and comparisons between various candidates from different disciplines. Over the years different trends in the awards can be traced. To a certain degree, the Nobel Prizes reflect the prevailing values of the day. In this way, they provide an interesting glimpse into the history of science, literature and peace work.

Historically, the distribution of the prizes is uneven. From a geographical viewpoint, Europe and North America are overrepresented. Alfred Nobel expressly stated that no consideration was to be made regarding nationality, but his ideas were rooted in the Western tradition of ideas. Modern science has had its strongest bastions in Europe and North America, and even though science today is more widespread, the research also requires greater resources. This has made it difficult for poorer countries to assert themselves in the world of science. Western authors and peace workers are overrepresented in literature and peace work as well. Here it is more difficult to find explanations in the traditions of ideas and economic resources.

The distribution between women and men shows another lack of balance. Part of the explanation lies in the fact that science was long dominated almost entirely by men. Women's opportunities for higher education have been strongly limited in many countries. Yet even today when women scientists have become more numerous,

In 1964 Jean-Paul Sartre became the first Nobel Laureate who voluntarily declined the prize.

A woman left out? One of the most debated Nobel Prizes is the chemistry prize of 1944. It was awarded to Otto Hahn for the discovery of fission of atomic nuclei. Many have argued that Lise Meitner, a physicist who had worked with Hahn in this and many other projects, also should have been recognized. The photograph depicts Meitner and Hahn in their laboratory in Dahlem outside of Berlin in 1913.

A Weird Insult from Norway

During the tensest hours of the Castro missile showdown a year ago this week, one American voice was heard in loud protest against President Kennedy's firm stand. "Horrifying . . . warlike . . . recklessly militaristic," said Caltech's chemist Dr. Linus Carl Pauling.

Headline in Life Magazine after the Nobel Peace Prize was awarded to Linus Pauling in 1963. Pauling's fight against nuclear tests was not popular in all quarters in his native United States.

they are hidden in obscurity. In the case of literature, it is even more difficult to find explanations for the comparatively lower numbers of women laureates. The area that has the most female Nobel Laureates is peace. The peace movement was the first political arena where women played an active role. The percentage of female peace prize recipients has not increased appreciably during the 1900s.

Over the years, the Nobel Prize has also been the object of other criticisms. For obvious reasons, the Peace Prize in particular has been politically controversial. At times, conflicts have arisen over whether the right person was named, and sometimes it has been claimed that worthy colleagues of the prize recipient were passed over. That the prizes in the natural sciences is only awarded to individuals has also been questioned in era when much scientific work is done by large teams.

The phenomenon of the Nobel Prizes in general has also been questioned. It has been argued that all such awards unavoidably corrupt the recipient. Several Nobel Laureates have claimed that prizes and honors draw unwanted attention that disturbs their life and work.

Alfred Nobel's intentions have not always been easy to fulfill. The stipulation in the will that the discovery or achievement shall have been made during the previous year has been given a very loose interpretation—it has been taken to mean that the importance of the discovery shall have been recently recognized.

The Nobel Prizes reflect the interests of Alfred Nobel the man, as well as those of a bygone era. Over the course of the years, many suggestions have been submitted for the establishment of new Nobel Prizes, including prizes in mathematics, environmental protection, and technology. In 1968 the Bank of Sweden established the Prize in Economic Sciences in Memory of Alfred Nobel, the only new prize in the context of the Nobel Prizes. The Nobel Foundation has decided that no additional prizes will be established.

Although the Nobel Prizes have been criticized, there has been no reduction of their fame and significance. Rather, the prestige of the Nobel Prizes accounts for the fact that so much energy has been devoted to questioning them.

Alone with his thoughts: Albert Einstein taking a walk at Princeton University in the mid-1950s. Einstein's original thinking revolutionized the world view of modern physics. His special theory of relativity from 1905 and general theory of relativity from 1915 radically transformed conceptions of time and space. Physicists had stated that the speed of light seemed to be constant for all observers, even if the light source was in motion. In order to keep this in agreement with their understanding of time and

space as absolute and constant, physicists utilized diverse theoretical constructions. Einstein took the opposite approach. He assumed that the speed of light was constant, and concluded that time and space are relative. This theory proved to hold true. Time and space were not the immovable entities they had been held to be.

Einstein's work on the photoelectric effect from 1905 was one of the most important steps toward the new world view brought on by quantum physics.

Matter as well as light are different forms of energy which can be transformed into one another in certain quantities, known as *quanta*. The universe is discrete in nature.

Albert Einstein received the 1921 Nobel Prize in Physics for his theory on the photoelectric effect. At this time, there was still disagreement regarding the theory of relativity, and it was made clear that Einstein did not primarily receive the prize for his work in that area.

A sense of intensity and creative urge is vibrant in Maggi Hambling's portrait of Dorothy Crowfoot Hodgkin in her office. Crowfoot Hodgkin discovered the structures of many biologically important substances by X-ray crystallography. For this she was awarded the Nobel Prize in Chemistry in 1964.

Individual Creativity

"Invention," "discovery," "improvement"—these words, which Alfred Nobel used in his will, pique our curiosity. Alfred Nobel wanted to reward the contributions of creative people. How does creative work come about? A look at the various paths Nobel laureates have followed to achieve their successes may shed some light on this question.

Perhaps we should begin with a more basic question: what do we mean by creativity? The basis of creativity is achieving something that did not exist previously, breaking down established patterns, seeing things in a new way.

But what drives people to achieve something new? How does the creative process work?

The origins of creativity vary greatly. The will or desire to create is often rooted in a person's innermost being. But what is creativity about? Anger and rebellion? Irresistible curiosity? Care for one's fellow human beings? A spirit of competition or sheer ambition? Happiness, desire, or obsession with one's work? Relief from pain and anguish?

The creative process may manifest itself in different ways. It can be a playful game or a stubborn battle. Sometimes it comes like a quick, burning insight or sudden inspiration. But often a groundbreaking achievement is preceded by long, patient work. Can the workings of the unconscious mind suddenly bring forth insight?

Sometimes it seems as though a new discovery arises unexpectedly by chance. Can we say that a seemingly coincidental discovery is creativity? Discoveries that at first seem mere chance often reveal themselves to be the fruit of careful and ingenious preparation. Even seemingly coincidental discoveries may necessitate lengthy interpretive work.

Creativity seldom springs out of nothingness. On the contrary, a creative innovation is a new combination of things that already exist. It may be the bridging or melding of knowledge or literary traditions. Or it may be a matter of putting previous experiences into a new context.

Even for individual creativity, the surrounding environment is significant. Does creative work occur best in lonely isolation or in exchanges with colleagues? Does loneliness sharpen concentration? Does isolation increase the powers of imagination? Can cooperation stimulate the thinking of the individual?

The following section deals with the creative work of a number of Nobel laureates. These are not necessarily stories of laureates whose work has yielded the most useful and important results for humanity and science. Rather, the stories of the laureates presented illustrate different aspects of human creativity. Many interesting and significant events in their lives have been omitted. Our focus is creativity, the creative process, and the driving forces behind it. Certainly, some important aspects of the creative work of many of these Nobel Prize recipients have been overlooked. These stories attempt to capture something of their work and the processes behind creative innovation in science, literature, and peace work.

Balance damped by air with microscopically readable
micrometer scale, designed according to guidelines by Pierre
Curie 1889. The damping makes the scale pans stop quickly.
The micrometer scale can be read with the microscope and the
mass calculated by a formula. Marie Curie used a balance of
this type when she determined the atomic weight of the newly
discovered element radium with high precision in 1907. The
chemical compounds that were to be weighed absorb steam
from the air and change their weight. To achieve high precision
it was therefore necessary that the weighing be done quickly.

Against the current

Marie Curie

Perhaps one of the most characteristic traits of a creative person is the ability to go one's own way. Marie Curie had an ability to break with convention and go against the mainstream, not only as an innovative scientist, but also as a woman in a world dominated by men.

Together with her husband Pierre, Marie Curie made discoveries that changed the way the world thought about the fundamental principles of matter. Their work led to knowledge that would be used for both good and evil, in applications ranging from cancer treatment to the atom bomb.

Marie Curie studied the radiation released by uranium, which had first been noted by Henri Becquerel in 1896. Curie observed that the levels of this radiation were the same regardless of the physical state of the uranium or what sort of chemical combination it might be found in. She concluded that the radiation emanated directly from uranium atoms themselves. Further, she deduced that since these atoms could emit radiation, they were not indivisible. This conflicted with earlier theories about atoms—the word "atom" itself means "indivisible."

In their continued research, Marie and Pierre Curie discovered that the ore known as pitchblende was more radioactive than pure uranium and thorium, two of the radioactive elements that it contains. Since the higher levels of radiation could not have been caused by the combination of these two elements, they theorized that the ore must contain yet other previously unknown radioactive elements. Isolating these new elements required enormous amounts of work. Sack by sack, the Curies stubbornly dragged to their laboratory tons of

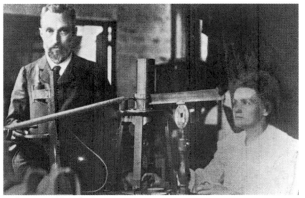
Pierre and Marie Curie

pitchblende, from which they were able to obtain small amounts of the new elements radium and polonium.

Traditional accounts of Marie Curie depict her as a person entirely devoted to her research, barely interested in the world outside her laboratory walls. This is an unfair characterization. In addition to her research, she saw to it that her discoveries found practical applications in medicine and industry. She did so not out of selfish economic interests, but with an idealistic belief in the possibilities that scientific research could provide for society. Curie's active cooperation with medicine and industry further enrich the image of her as one of the most unique pioneering sciencists of the 20th century.

o Marie and Pierre Curie, Nobel Prize in Physics, 1903. Marie Curie, Nobel Prize in Chemistry, 1911.

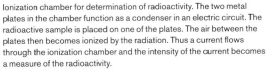

Ionization chamber for determination of radioactivity. The two metal plates in the chamber function as a condenser in an electric circuit. The radioactive sample is placed on one of the plates. The air between the plates then becomes ionized by the radiation. Thus a current flows through the ionization chamber and the intensity of the current becomes a measure of the radioactivity.

In order to measure the radioactivity quantitatively, Pierre and Marie Curie in 1898 designed a simple ionization chamber that was driven by a battery and connected to an electrometer. This was compensated by a current from a piezoelectrical balance. The weight that had to be placed in the scale pan was the measure of the radioactivity.

< Marie Curie in her laboratory circa 1913.

< Advertisement for radium salts and other radioactive substances. Marie Curie was an enterprising woman and herself took part in the industrial application of her scientific results.

The staging of *Waiting for Godot* at Théatre Hébertot in June 1956: Lucien Raimbourg, Samuel Beckett, Pierre Latour, Jean Martin, Roger Blin, Albert Rémy.

Exploring the zone of being

Samuel Beckett

Samuel Beckett's early books were filled with puns and literary humor in the style of fellow Irishman James Joyce's works. In order to become a creative author in his own right, Beckett had to free himself from these established patterns. He managed to do this, and by 1956, when he compared himself to Joyce, he could point out the differences rather than the similarities in their work. While Joyce was a master of language, Beckett had moved in another direction:

"He's tending towards omniscience and omnipotence as an artist. I'm working with impotence, ignorance. There seems to be a kind of aesthetic axiom that expression is achievement—must be achievement. My little exploration is that whole zone of being that has always been set aside by the artist as something unusable—as something incompatible with art."

Beckett sought out the most basic conditions of our existence in order to understand the meaning of life. His plays became more and more ritualistic and their dialogue more sparse. Finally, he began to doubt the value of language itself, and his plays bordered on silence.

Beckett is one of a number of Irish writers who worked outside Ireland. He had met James Joyce in 1928 in Paris, where he had gone to study and teach. During WWII, Beckett was a member of the French resistance movement against the Nazis. After the war he returned to Paris from Normandy. It was at this time that he began to write in French. This proved to be an enormous liberation for Beckett. He found French to be a practical and straightforward language of concrete meanings. Beckett claimed that, in French, it was easier for him to "write without style."

A laughing Samuel Beckett. Beckett was not only a writer who emphasized silence and barrenness, but also one who displayed humour.

Beckett's experiences during the war—uncertainty, confusion, exile, hunger, and poverty—had a great effect upon his writing. His return to Paris was the beginning of a period of incredible creativity, which he later referred to as "the siege in the room." In the spring of 1946, during a visit to Dublin, Beckett experienced another period of intense creativity after a revelation that he should allow existential problems to come to the forefront of his work. Writing at night, working in an almost trance-like state, in the short space of four months Beckett produced four novels, two plays, essays, criticism, and a collection of short stories.

o Samuel Beckett, Nobel Prize in Literature, 1969.

Even in today's world the Dalai Lama gathers wisdom
and inspiration from a sutra with old Buddhist texts.

Glasses of the type the Dalai Lama uses.

Distant horizons

Tenzin Gyatso, the Fourteenth Dalai Lama of Tibet

One of the first features one notices about Tenzin Gyatso, the Fourteenth Dalai Lama of Tibet, is his glasses. Does the Dalai Lama see this world differently than others?

The nations surrounding Tibet have found it easy to dismiss Tibetan culture as ancient myths and legends with little power to influence change in the world of today. For the Dalai Lama, religion became the foremost weapon in the struggle against communist Chinese occupation of Tibet.

The Dalai Lama was born to the role of a leader. According to Tibetan Buddhist tradition, the Dalai Lama is reincarnated. When the thirteenth Dalai Lama died, the search was begun for the boy who would be the fourteenth Dalai Lama. A little boy named Tenzin Gyatso was found to be the new leader. Today he is the leader of the Tibetan people, not only spiritually, but also politically. Tibet is occupied by China, and has been the scene of many violent conflicts. Since 1959, the Dalai Lama has lived in exile in India.

For the Dalai Lama, the cultivation of inner peace and integrity is the ultimate weapon for achieving positive change in an irrational world. Tolerance and understanding are the key components in his world view.

In 1987, the Dalai Lama presented his plan for peace. Under this plan, Tibet would be declared a neutral zone. He calls for the creation of "a sanctuary of peace and a resource of spiritual inspiration at the heart of Asia." The plan is innovative in terms of the central role it gives to care of the environment.

In the Dalai Lama's thinking, human reason is limitless. He has been interested in science and technology

since he was very young. He is fond of quoting Buddha, who said that it is our duty to examine the world with logic and reason, rather than relying on faith alone.

o The fourteenth Dalai Lama, Nobel Peace Prize, 1989.

Different perspectives

Amartya Sen

Amartya Sen's old teacher at Santiniketan said that his former student was "a boy of promise, but never bookish." There were too many important things outside school for him to be interested in. In the outlying villages poverty and illiteracy were rampant. At 14 years of age Amartya Sen became secretary of the student council's social work committee, and started schools for the village children. Of course, instruction could only be given when he himself did not have to be in school: during physical education classes, or in the evenings. Some of Sen's classmates and teachers also became involved in these schools. "His zeal was indeed infectious," said his teacher.

This desire to improve conditions for the poorest of the poor runs like a golden thread through Amartya Sen's life, and has led him to look at common problems in a new way. As a child, he witnessed a disastrous famine in Bengal during which millions of people starved to death. Yet his family and classmates from the middle class suffered no want of food. Quite simply, the famine afflicted only the poorest. How could famine occur in a region where there was actually plenty of food? The question led Sen to study the nature of poverty, and how a society's resources are distributed. Sen's investigation of poverty brings out the critical role of the opportunities that the society offers to the individual. Health and education are key factors, in addition to economic relations.

This has led him to investigate how democracy functions, and how its paradoxes and impossibilities can be resolved. Sen has also worked to find ways in which social

Amartya Sen and Emma Rothschild in Stockholm for the Nobel festivities, 1998.

choice and political decisions can accommodate individual rights.

But Amartya Sen is not only a theoretician. He has also performed practical work, including a study on differences between baby girls and boys. As a world-renowned professor of economics, he employed an assistant to weigh the children. Problems arose when the children did not want to be weighed, and bit the assistant. The episode ended with Amartya Sen bicycling through the countryside of West Bengal, weighing the children himself. With a delighted laugh he explains, "As a father of four, I have a certain amount of experience."
o Amartya Sen, the Bank of Sweden Prize in Economic Sciences in Memory of Alfred Nobel, 1998.

‹ Amartya Sen on a research trip on his bicycle.

This so-called "samizdat" booklet with "Jurij Zhivago's poems" was written in the late 1940s. Booklets like this were circulated in the Soviet Union when the novel was banned. In the booklet there are notes by Pasternak's first wife Evgenia Vladimirovna Pasternak.

Метельмихла на стекле
Кружки и стрелы.
Свеча горела на столе,
Свеча горела.

Порывом вьюги из угла
Порыв соблазна
Вздымал, как ангел, два крыла
Крестообразно.

Мело метель по всей земле,
Во все пределы.
Свеча горела на столе,
Свеча горела.

10

Poetry as a force of nature

Boris Pasternak

In the summer of 1917, Boris Pasternak wrote a collection of love poems that he titled *My Sister, Life*. The spontaneous lyrics of this work broke down boundaries and over-rode common notions. The contours of the modern city, images of nature, and a whole range of literary allusions were rearranged and remolded into a dynamic picture of the world reborn. The collection makes use of everyday language, lending it the glow of confessions of love. According to Pasternak, creativity was a matter of a special "temperature" in reality, as experienced by the artist.

Boris Pasternak was a product of the seething spiritual and artistic environment of Moscow around the time of the first Russian revolution of 1905. He came from a family of two artists: his father was a painter, and his mother a concert pianist. Pasternak studied music composition and began composing at age thirteen. Although he chose not to become a professional musician, music remained an important source of inspiration to him later in life.

In his autobiographical work *Safe Conduct*, Pasternak describes his childhood home and growing-up years in Moscow. The book shows Pasternak's ties to his own cultural heritage of pre-Soviet Russia and the European tradition. *Safe Conduct* is also a reply to the Soviet Union's immovable official cultural doctrine of "socialistic realism" formulated in the 1930s. Pasternak struggled to avoid writing for the cause of "the social order." The letter of safe conduct referred to in the title was to protect the poet during his "journey" through Soviet culture.

During the second half of the 1940s, Pasternak began to write his great novel, *Doctor Zhivago*. In the 1950s he moved to the writer's village of Peredelkino; in nature

and in the simple life around his home there he found strength and inspiration to complete the novel. Refused for publication locally, *Doctor Zhivago* was subsequently published in the West, heralding a Soviet campaign of persecution against the author.

In liberal and dissident circles, Pasternak's work was much appreciated. *Doctor Zhivago* was smuggled in from the West or circulated in illegal typewritten copies. As early as the 1940s, readings of chapters from the novel were organized in private homes in Moscow.

In his homeland, Pasternak was already loved as a poet. Yet it was not until the Perestroika period of the late 1980s that *Doctor Zhivago* could be published in Russia, making him known to the Russian people as a great novelist as well.

o Boris Pasternak, Nobel Prize in Literature, 1958.

Boris Pasternak as a young boy with his parents Leonid and Rosa. At the right in the family photograph below is Boris's brother Alexander.

Pasternak with fellow authors in 1925. In the front row are Pasternak, Viktor Shlovsky, Sergej Tretjakov, and Vladimir Mayakovsky. In the back row are P. Nezmanov and Osip Brik.

After the announcement of the Nobel Prize in 1958, Pasternak was congratulated by author Korney Chukovsky and other friends. Pasternak was at first overjoyed. After receiving pressure from the authorities, he was forced to decline the prize. In the first stanza of a poem entitled "The Nobel Prize," he wrote:

I'm caught like a beast in a trap,
Somewhere there's freedom, people, light,
But the hunt is after me,
And there's no way out.

Pasternak in his study.

The beret became one of the distinctive features of the
radical chemist and champion of peace Linus Pauling.

Anti-war crusader

Linus Pauling

Linus Pauling's engagement in social issues began when the first atom bomb was dropped over Hiroshima. His concern, anger, and indignation at the threat of nuclear weapons changed his own life forever, and even influenced world opinion.

At the start of WWII, Pauling was already a prominent chemist. His achievements in that area are dealt with in a later section of this book. Like many other scientists, he worked on a number of projects related to the war effort, from blood replacement materials to explosives. He was also asked to work on the atomic bomb project, but declined because he had too much other work to do. It was not until the first bomb was dropped that Pauling realized the horrible potential of this new weapon.

Pauling began a long campaign against atomic weapons and nuclear tests. He was strongly influenced by his wife Ava Helen, who had been involved in earlier peace work. It was Ava Helen who told Pauling that if he were to maintain his credibility in the public debate, he would need prodigious knowledge about all areas covered by these issues. He decided to spend half of his time examining the social, economic and political aspects of nuclear weapons.

Pauling's engagement in these issues made his life difficult. He was suspected of being a communist sympathizer and was interrogated in the McCarthy hearings. Pauling's passport was confiscated. This prohibited him from traveling and working with colleagues abroad.

Nonetheless, because of Pauling, many other scientists took a stance against nuclear weapons testing. In a call for a ban on tests, he succeeded in gathering 11,021 signatures, which were forwarded to the UN. He participated in protests and made statements in the press. He wrote letters and sent telegrams to President John F. Kennedy and to Soviet leader Khrushchev, asking them to accept a ban. Pauling's efforts were not in vain—an agreement declaring a freeze on nuclear weapons was signed in 1963.

His involvement in public issues and his straightforward way of expressing his opinions often put Linus Pauling under pressure. The artsy-looking beret that he often wore added to his radical image. Actually, Pauling did not enjoy controversy—he said it disturbed his work.
o Linus Pauling, Nobel Peace Prize, 1963.

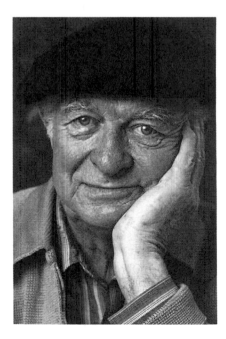

Linus Pauling demonstrating against nuclear tests.

Linus Pauling on a visit to Sweden with his wife Ava Helen by his side. Ava Helen Pauling played an important part in her husband's commitment to peace. When Linus Pauling accepted the peace prize, he said he would have preferred that the prize could be shared with his wife.

"Femtoland" is Ahmed Zewail's name for his laboratory. There the details of chemical reactions can be studied with laser equipment.

A passion for discovery

Ahmed Zewail

Even as a small boy in Egypt, Ahmed Zewail had a passion for science. From a few glass tubes and the oil stove that his mother used to make coffee, he constructed a small apparatus in his bedroom to see how wood could be transformed into flammable gases and liquids. The experiment is etched into Zewail's mind, not only as an early foray into science, but also because his mother was afraid he would burn down the house.

The excitement and total enchantment he felt as a child remain powerful forces in Zewail's life. His research centers around how chemical reactions occur. Using laser technology, he has developed a method of "photography" utilizing "shutter times" as short as a femtosecond, or .000000000000001 second. A sign above the door to his laboratory reads "Femtoland." Here Zewail captures images of chemical reactions in exquisite detail. With his femtoscope, Zewail has made studies of literally everything that moves in the world of invisible molecules, just as Galileo's telescope brought into view the very far, then-invisible universe. As a boy experimenting in his bedroom, he had yet to dream that he would one day uncover the mystery of how matter is transformed from one substance to another.

As a young researcher at the University of Alexandria, Zewail found joy and satisfaction in explaining natural phenomena in clear, straightforward ways. He remains convinced that for each and every universal phenomenon, it is possible to develop a description that is both simple and beautiful.

Zewail has a penchant for metaphors. In describing his research, he usually begins by saying that a femtosecond

Ahmed Zewail as a young boy.

is to one second as a second is to 32 million years. He speaks of chemical reactions in terms of atoms that marry and then divorce one another. His work is like making a 32 million year-long film and then viewing it second by second—a femtomovie.

Like most scientists today, Ahmed Zewail finds his surroundings and colleagues of great importance. At his home institution at the California Institute of Technology in Pasadena, Zewail speaks of his "scientific family," whose members come from around the world, bringing with them different backgrounds, cultures, and skills. This globalization of human knowledge, Zewail said in his Nobel Lecture, is key to progress, unity, and optimism.

o Ahmed Zewail, Nobel Prize in Chemistry, 1999.

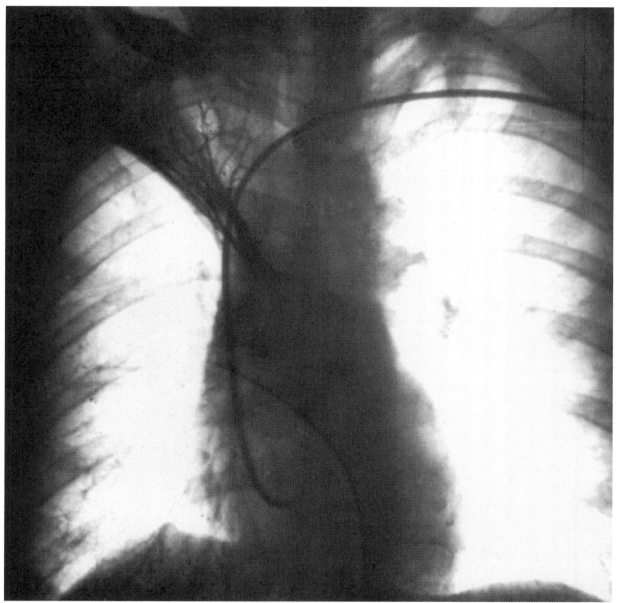

X-ray photograph of heart catheterization. The first heart catheterization was performed in 1929 by Werner Forssmann on himself.

The risks of curiosity

Werner Forssmann

The heart is the pulsing source of life, beating on whether we will it or not. In human consciousness, the heart also plays a very important symbolic role. It represents not only our innermost thoughts and emotions, but also our vulnerability. The thought of touching or experimenting with a beating heart gives most of us a feeling of discomfort—to say the least. Those with a burning desire to learn may conquer their feelings of uneasiness, even if they must put their own life at risk to do so.

In 1929, a young German doctor named Werner Forssmann was fascinated by an account of an experiment performed on a horse. A tube had been passed through a vein into the horse's heart. A small balloon fastened to the other end of the tube showed how the pressure within the heart fluctuated. Forssmann became convinced that the same procedure could be performed on a human being, thereby providing important new information about the functioning of the heart.

At the hospital where he worked, Forssmann told his supervisor about his idea. The supervisor forbid him to perform such an experiment, certain that the risk to the patient would be far too great. Forssmann then asked that the experiment be performed on him, and was again told that this would not be allowed.

Forssmann decided to defy his orders and perform the experiment on himself in secret. He inserted a catheter into the crook of his arm. He then went down to the x-ray room in the hospital cellar. On the x-ray screen, he could see the catheter in his arm, and continued to insert it into his body. At last, the catheter entered his heart. As proof of what he done, he took and published an x-ray photograph.

Werner Forssmann, in the middle, surrounded by André Cournand and Dickinson Richards, with whom he shared the Nobel Prize.

Many in the medical establishment felt that Forssmann's experiment was of scientific importance. Yet his actions also damaged his standing as a doctor. Some people saw him as unstable and even dangerous. The famous Charité Hospital in Berlin dismissed him with the statement that "You might lecture in a circus about your little tricks, but never in a respectable German university!"

The resistance to his work made Forssmann give up his dreams of being a researcher. The recognition he received later in life came as a surprise. He felt that he was just another general practitioner among many thousands of doctors. When he received the Nobel prize, he told a reporter, "I feel like the village parson who has just learned that he has been made bishop."

o Werner Forssmann, Nobel Prize in Physiology or Medicine, 1956.

Maize ears carrying the transposable elements "Ac" (activator) and "Spm" (suppressor-mutator). The ear at the top carries a2-ml, a Spm-induced mutation in a color gene. Spm is also segregating, resulting in some spotted and some non-spotted kernels. The ear below carries Ac at the Bronze gene, resulting in bronze kernels with purple spots.

Unique relationships

Barbara McClintock

Barbara McClintock's creative research on genetic inheritance literally began out in the field, among cornstalks. In the laboratory, she peered through her microscope and imagined that she was down in there, walking between the chromosomes. The capacity to devote herself to her task with a sense of fun and vivid insight was one of McClintock's most unusual characteristics.

McClintock found that genes could reposition themselves on chromosomes, and that organisms had developed processes to control the functions of their genes. Her discovery that the genetic elements were not stable and unmoving conflicted with the prevalent views of the day. When McClintock first presented her results, she was already a respected researcher. However, her colleagues were skeptical and even cool to her claims of "jumping genes." McClintock was years ahead of her time in her research and thinking. It would be several decades before other scientists would agree with her understanding of hereditary processes.

Not until the 1970s did it become clear that "jumping genes" are not unique to corn plants. They exist in all living organisms, from simple bacteria to human beings, and are nature's way of creating genetic variations.

What allowed Barbara McClintock to see farther and deeper than her colleagues? Again and again, she stated that a researcher must take the time to look, have the patience to "hear what the material has to say to you," and be open to what is in front of you. Most importantly, the researcher must have respect for life. It would not be entirely correct to call Barbara McClintock a mystic, but she did have a way of seeing living organisms in a differ-

Barbara McClintock at her microscope.

ent way than her colleagues did. She felt a tie to all living things—cells, organisms, and the entire ecosystem.

Some of McClintock's fellow researchers felt that research on corn was far too slow. At best, corn can be harvested twice a year, while microorganisms reproduce in just a few minutes. For Barbara McClintock this was an advantage, since it gave her time for the analyses and insights necessary for a deeper understanding of her work.

o Barbara McClintock, Nobel Prize in Physiology or Medicine, 1983.

Barbara McClintock, at the far right, with other cytogeneticists at Cornell University: C. Burnham, M. Rhoades, R. Emerson, George Beadle.

Barbara McClintock nursed and studied her maize plants out in the fields.

One of the things Nelly
Sachs brought to Sweden
when she escaped from
Nazi Berlin was a music box.

From the depth of despair

Nelly Sachs

A music box—a seemingly insignificant item in and of itself and yet invested with an aura of inspiration and a sense of security. While the driving force behind the work of Nelly Sachs was the great sorrow and suffering she had known, small, ordinary items seemed to console and inspire her in her writing.

Nelly Sachs was born into a Jewish family in Berlin. She lived there until Nazi persecution forced her to flee on the last passenger airline flight out of Germany in 1940. In Stockholm, Sweden she made a new home for herself, settling into a small apartment filled with furniture and mementos. She found herself alone, a foreigner and a refugee, living among several cultures—German, Jewish, and Swedish. She combined influences from each of these cultures in her authorship.

Sachs was innovative in her combination of a mystic-religious vision with modernistic structures. The dark undertones of her poetry are not unusual for the creative spirit. In her youth, a doctor advised her to work through her sorrow—then being experienced because of a deep and unhappy love—by writing. Later in life, she wrote in the same way to survive her awareness of the Holocaust. The fate of her loved ones and of the Jewish people became the source of her work: "Death was my teacher, metaphors are my wounds."

The poetry of Nelly Sachs is a monument to the suffering of a people. It is immense and fearsome in scope, yet fragile, and reveals glimpses of hope. The visionary tone is punctuated by concrete references that hint at the inspiration Sachs found in rather ordinary objects.

Nelly Sachs with Swedish fellow authors Artur Lundkvist and Erik Lindegren.

Der Spinozaforscher
H.H.

Du last und hieltest eine Muschel in der Hand
Der Abend kam mit zarter Abschiedsrose.
Dein Zimmer wurde mit der Ewigkeit bekannt
Und die Musik begann in einer alten Dose.

Der leuchter brannte in dem Abendschein;
Du branntest von der fernen Segnung.
Die Eiche seufzte aus dem Ahnenschrein
Und das Vergangne feierte Begegnung.

o Nelly Sachs, Nobel Prize in Literature, 1966.

Devotion and forsaking

Aung San Suu Kyi

Achieving great results often requires uncompromising devotion to one's cause. It is such devotion to her cause that drives Aung San Suu Kyi. Suu Kyi is the daughter of Aung San, Burma's national hero, who led the struggle for freedom, first against the British colonial powers and then against Japanese occupation forces. Aung San was murdered in 1947 when his daughter was only two years old.

Although Aung San Suu Kyi inherited a distinguished family name, she lived in anonymity for many years. She has spent most of her life outside Burma, living mostly in England, married to Englishman Michel Aris.

During an eight-month period before her marriage, she wrote 187 letters to her fiancé and repeatedly expressed her concern that the marriage would be misunderstood by her people and her family as a lack of interest in them. She repeated that one day she would be forced to return to Burma: "I only ask one thing, that should my people need me, you would help me to do my duty by them."

In 1988 Aung San Suu Kyi traveled to Burma in order to care for her mother, who had become seriously ill. For some time before that, demands for reform in Burma had been gaining momentum. Students protested in the streets and there were outbreaks of violence. Burma's leader, Ne Win announced that a referendum would be held to decide the country's future. A military junta then seized power, promising a transition to democracy. However, the violence continued. Suu Kyi decided to enter the fight for freedom. When the junta put her under house arrest she went on a hunger strike.

In 1990, general elections were introduced. The elections were won by the National League for Democracy

Aung San Suu Kyi leaving flowers at her father's mausoleum in 1995.

party, which Suu Kyi had helped to start, but the junta refused to release its power. Suu Kyi continued to be held in isolation. Eventually, her husband and their two sons were allowed to visit her. In 1995, she was finally released from house arrest. However, she has not left Burma because she has not been given any guarantee that she would be permitted to return. Because of this, she was not even able to visit her husband when he lay on his deathbed.

When asked if it wasn't difficult to forsake her family, Aung San Suu Kyi replied that she did not feel that she had any choice. For Suu Kyi, her father, her homeland, and her family are one and the same. Doing her duty and being true to her cause was a necessity.

o Aung San Suu Kyi, Nobel Peace Prize, 1991.

The emptiness between the words

Yasunari Kawabata

Yasunari Kawabata's calligraphy is characterized by a pure, simple beauty. Kawabata favored an austere esthetic. Regarding ink painting, he said: "The heart of the ink painting is in space, abbreviation, what is left undrawn."

As a youth, Kawabata at first wanted to be a painter, but his interest in literature was awakened early on. A journal that he kept until he was fifteen was later reworked into one of his first novels. Its contents give witness to the feelings of sorrow and loneliness that marked his childhood. When Kawabata was only a few days old both of his parents died, and he grew up on an isolated farm with his maternal grandparents. A melancholy mood came to characterize his future production.

After studying literature at a university, Kawabata

Kawabata in his study in Kamakura.

found his way into the circle of writers involved in the newly established magazine *Bundei-jidai*. The movement strove to create a new literature by combining modern Western currents with traditional Japanese literature. Kawabata, an authority in both areas, soon became a leading figure. His early work gives lively depictions of modern life in Tokyo. After WWII, Kawabata's writings drew further and further away from the bustle of the contemporary period. He came to see it as his task to preserve the beauty of the past in his works, and carry it over to the changing modern world. Ancient Japanese rituals and milieus were described in minute detail. The Japanese tea ceremony occupied a special place in Kawabata's stories—it contained a meditative quiet that was also important to his writing. He viewed artistic creation as a form of meditation in which the mind is emptied: "the emphasis is less upon reason and argument than upon intuition, immediate feeling."

Throughout his career as an author, Kawabata wrote what he called "palm-of-the-hand stories." He felt that these short prose pieces, often no longer than one or two pages, expressed the essence of his work. One of his last literary projects was to rework his novel *Snow Country* into a palm-of-the-hand story. This minimalist style of storytelling can be compared to a calligraphy master's sparse strokes on paper, which express a greater whole. The action in the stories is greatly reduced, but deals with the same themes as his larger works: loneliness, love, beauty, and death.

o Yasunari Kawabata, Nobel Prize in Literature, 1968.

An inner stillness
Dag Hammarskjöld

"The longest journey is the journey inwards." Thus begins one of Dag Hammarskjöld's poems in his posthumously published book *Markings*. Hammarskjöld was a meditative man, and for him, spirituality was more than a search for his own inner well-being. Rather, it gave him the strength he needed to be a creative problem solver for an uneasy and volatile world.

"To preserve the silence within—amid all the noise. To remain open and quiet, a moist humus in the fertile darkness where the rain falls and the grain ripens—no matter how many tramp across the parade ground in whirling dust under an arid sky."

Hammarskjöld often spent time in Sweden's natural areas in order to find tranquility. However, he sought peace and quiet wherever he found himself. At the UN headquarters, he oversaw the rebuilding of the meditation room. Hammarskjöld felt that "a room of stillness" was needed, because "when we come to our own deepest feelings and urgings we have to be alone, we have to feel the sky and the earth and hear the voice that speaks within us."

Hammarskjöld found strength in introspection. His work was characterized by enormous energy and strict discipline. He seldom did anything unnecessarily. He concentrated on one task at a time, and there was rarely more than one piece of paper on his desk at any given time.

Hammarskjöld himself confessed that his self-discipline did contain a certain amount of egoism. He sometimes offended people by his brusque manner.

‹ The meditation room at the UN headquarters in New York: "This is a room devoted to peace and those who are giving their lives for peace. It is a room of quiet where only thoughts should speak."

Hammarskjöld's strengths were most obvious during the Belgian Congo crisis. The Soviet Union accused Hammarskjöld of supporting the imperialist interests of the United States. In a dramatic speech, Soviet leader Nikita Khrushchev demanded that he resign. Yet Hammarskjöld refused to bow before the Soviet Union or any other superpower. He believed that he had been called to protect the other nations of the world, those that truly needed protection: "I shall remain in my post during the term of my office as a servant of the Organization in the interest of all those other nations, as long as they wish me to do so."

However, Hammarskjöld was not to remain at his post until the end of his term. In September 1961, he was killed in an airplane crash while enroute to peace negotiations in the Congo.

o Dag Hammarskjöld, Nobel Peace Prize, 1961.

Mountaineer's axe given to Dag Hammarskjöld by the Mount Everest climber Sherpa Tensing. The inscription reads:
To his excellency Dag Hammarskjöld, Secretary General of the United Nations "so you may climb to even greater heights"
Sherpa Tensing
June 1954

Dag Hammarskjöld was a devoted photographer and mountaineer. Perhaps his endurance and stubbornness is mirrored in his interest in climbing. One of his aphorisms reads: "Never measure the height of a mountain until you have reached the top. Then you will see how low it was."

When Hammarskjöld sketched out an intricate solution to an organizational problem involving the UN's mediation work in the Congo conflict, he triumphantly wrote, "That's how!"

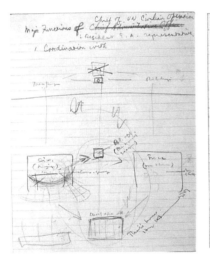

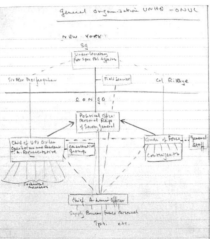

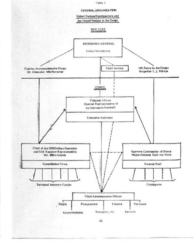

Isolation and influence

Hideki Yukawa

"The window of my little world opened out only to the garden of science, but from that window, enough light streamed in."

Physicist Hideki Yukawa's work is marked by an interplay between isolation and outside influences. In his autobiography, Yukawa describes himself as lonely, introverted, and silent, especially as a child. This was in part due to the complicated relationship he had with his father, but to other reasons as well. In the Kyoto of Yukawa's childhood, the houses were built so that their inhabitants were isolated from the world outside. Yukawa wrote that growing up in such a closed environment could foster a rich imagination and a romantic temperament in a child. As a student, it was not unusual for him to spend entire days reading periodicals, without exchanging a single word with anyone.

Yukawa's window onto the world of science was opened by colleagues who had studied the new physics while in Europe. One of these, Yoshio Nishina, had spent much time in Copenhagen as part of Niels Bohr's research group.

Yukawa's work focused on the forces that hold together the nucleus of an atom. Scientists understood that the nucleus was composed of protons and neutrons, but the mystery of how they were held within the nucleus remained unsolved. One theory proposed that there was a third particle that bound them together. Various solutions based on this idea had been proposed, but none held up to scrutiny.

< The four Ogawa brothers: Shigeki, Hideki, Tamaki, and Yoshiki. Hideki received the name Yukawa when he married.

Yukawa walking with Albert Einstein and others.

During 1934, Yukawa often lay awake at night thinking about this problem. He had a notebook at the side of his bed, so that he could record any thoughts that he might have. Sometimes he believed that he was close to a solution, but when he thought through his ideas in the morning, they proved to be worthless. One night, however, an insight came to him—there must be a relationship between the intensity of the force and the mass of the binding particle. On the basis of this idea, Yukawa calculated that this binding particle would have a mass 200 times that of an electron. He called this particle a "meson."

Yukawa's theory mapped out binding forces within the atomic nucleus that are enormous. Today we know that releasing these forces may have dire consequences. Yukawa had no idea that his work would lead to problems of so many types. Despite this, Yukawa felt that it was best to allow scientific work to go on unhindered by the concerns of a complicated world. However, Yukawa also worked for peace, particularly in the Pugwash movement. o Hideki Yukawa, Nobel Prize in Physics, 1949.

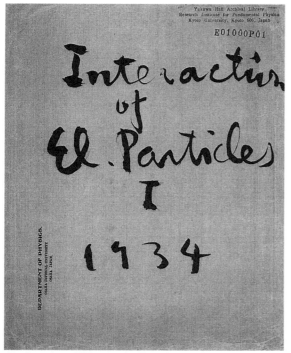

Envelope of one of Yukawa's scientific manuscripts.

Calligraphy by Hideki Yukawa with a painting by his wife Sumi Yukawa. Hideki Yukawa has written that he was never particularly good working with his hands when he went to school—this was one of his reasons for becoming a theoretical physicist. However, there was one handicraft he was good at—calligraphy. He had learned calligraphy at home from a teacher who had studied the art in China.

Hideki Yukawa, at the right in the top row, at Kyoto University. At the left in the top row is another future Nobel Laureate in physics, Sin-Itiro Tomonaga.

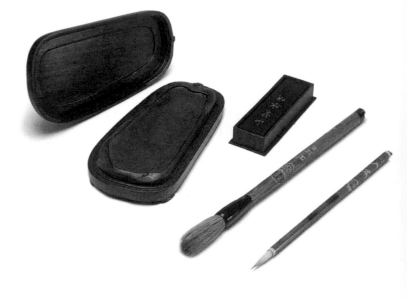

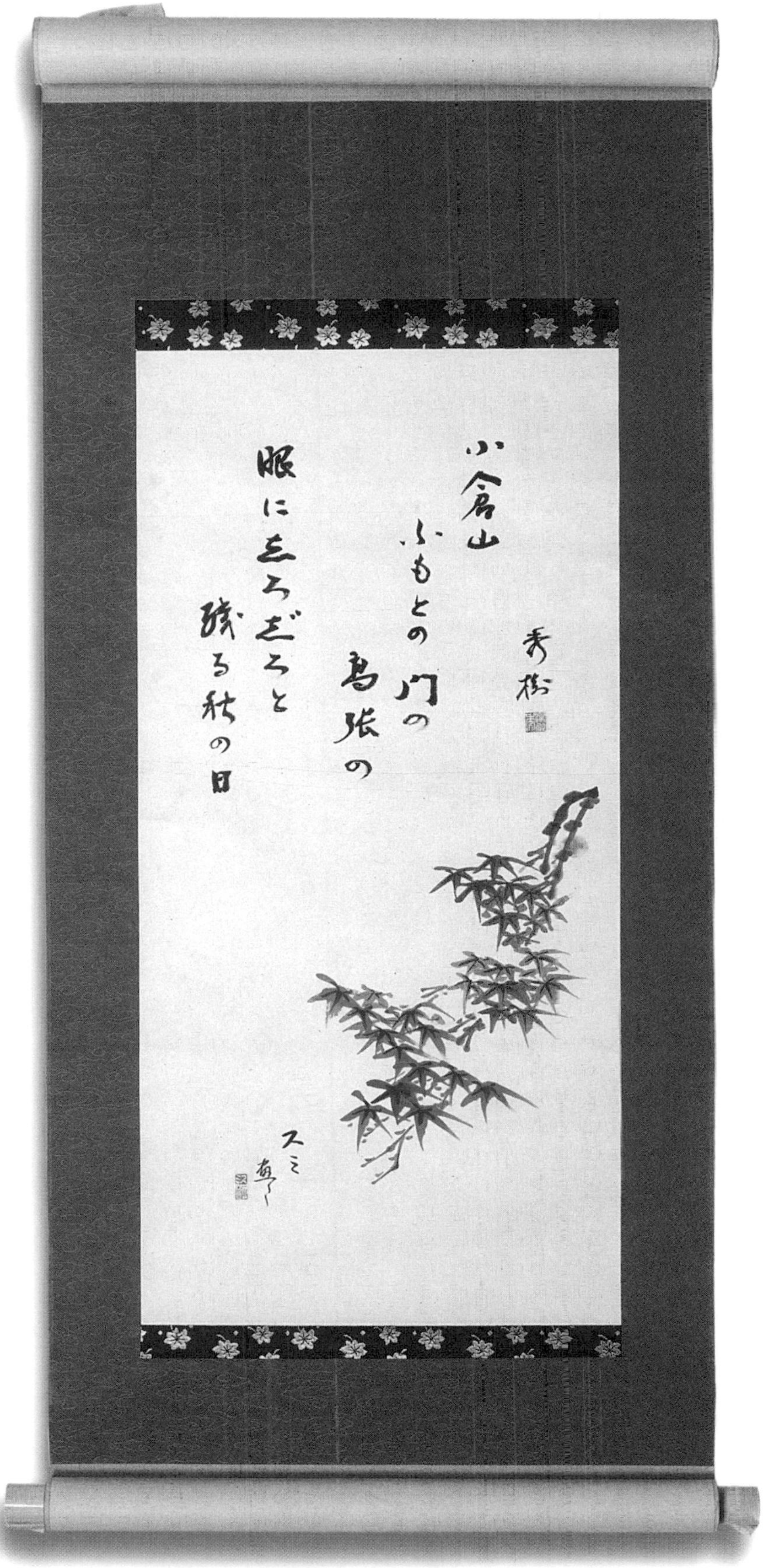

小倉山
ふもとの門の
秀樹
眼にゝろゝゝと
高張の
残る秋の日

Doing a full day's work

Ernest Hemingway

"Writing, at its best, is a lonely life. Organizations for writers palliate the writer's loneliness but I doubt if they improve his writing. He grows in public stature as he sheds his loneliness and often his work deteriorates. For he does his work alone and if he is a good enough writer he must face eternity, or the lack of it, each day.

For a true writer each book should be a new beginning where he tries again for something that is beyond attainment. He should always try for something that has never been done or that others have tried and failed."

Ernest Hemingway's characterization of creative authorship as a life of solitude may seem somewhat surprising. Hemingway is often associated with stimulating and inspiring activities—bullfighting, nights spent in bars and other pastimes in the company of good friends.

Yet Hemingway was also an energetic reader—he could read three books a day, and subscribed to half a dozen newspapers and twenty magazines. A patient practitioner of the writer's craft, he could rewrite an introductory chapter 40 or 50 times.

Hemingway usually began writing a new book in pencil on thin typewriter paper, clamped onto a clipboard. On a good day he used up seven pencils. At this stage, he used the typewriter only for work he found quick and easy to write, such as dialogues. But at the end of the day he reread everything and rewrote it. To see how the work as a whole was progressing, and to avoid fooling himself, he recorded the day's total production of words in a chart on a piece of cardboard he had pinned to the wall. On certain days, he might produce a higher word count in order

< Ernest Hemingway in the bookshop Shakespeare & Co in Paris.

to reward himself with a fishing trip the next day. Keeping his production high was not the only purpose of Hemingway's word counting. It was also a habit from his days as a correspondent, when it cost money to send in each word. It was important to make the text as interesting as possible for the cost.

Hemingway tried not to write for any more than six hours per day. After that, he became tired and the quality dropped. If he stopped while things were still going well he avoided the risk of becoming stuck. By setting aside his work until the next day, Hemingway could allow his subconscious mind to continue working without his brain becoming tired.

o Ernest Hemingway, Nobel Prize in Literature, 1954.

Isaac Bashevis Singer's Yiddish typewriter. Mainly derived from Medieval German, Yiddish is a language with many words borrowed from Hebrew and Slavic that is written in Hebrew characters.

Stick to your work!

Isaac Bashevis Singer

"Whatever happens, you stick to your work. I'll buy you a Yiddish typewriter." Isaac Bashevis Singer heard these words of encouragement from his brother just after he had arrived in New York in 1935. He soon had his Yiddish typewriter, and it became his faithful companion in a lifetime of unceasing writing and a never ending battle against writer's block.

Singer had grown up in a poor Jewish neighborhood in Warsaw. He fled to the United States after Hitler rose to power in Germany and began his campaign of increasing pressure on the Jews of Poland. Even after his move to New York, Singer continued to write in his mother tongue of Yiddish, the dominant language among the Jews of Europe from the Middle Ages to the WWII.

Mysticism and superstition played an important role in Singer's world. Even his typewriter seemed to be a living thing. He said that if it did not enjoy a story, it would stop working. For several years after he arrived in the United States, Singer suffered a terrible writer's block. He produced no fiction works during this time. He eventually overcame this block, but he always felt that it lurked threateningly close by. The typewriter helped him keep on writing: "Often I sit down and I don't know what I am going to write. But I do not abandon it because I have a very old Yiddish typewriter, it is 43 years old, and I don't want to insult it. So I stay and try to write."

Singer set the pattern for his regular habit of writing every day when he worked for newspapers, especially the *Jewish Daily Forward*:

"An artist, like a horse, needs a whip. I'm so accustomed to delivering stuff that it has become almost my

second nature. Now let me tell you, I haven't missed a week in all these years, except that I get four weeks' vacation. But then I work harder than ever in preparing copy for after the vacation."

Although writing became a routine task for Singer, his stories are full of life. The world that flowed out of his typewriter is populated by fantastical demons, sorcerers, fools, false prophets, rabbis, and marketplace madams.

The world that inspired Singer—the Jewish villages and ghettoes of central and eastern Europe—were destroyed during WWII. Through Singer's stories, that lost world lives on.

o Isaac Bashevis Singer, Nobel Prize in Literature, 1978.

Illustrations for Singer's stories "A Tale of Two Liars" and "The Spinoza of Market Street" by Sylvia Ary.

Endurance and reconciliation

Nelson Mandela

One day in 1990, after 27 years in prison, Nelson Mandela stepped out into freedom. The following year he was elected president of South Africa. The world was amazed that Mandela had been able to endure his lengthy imprisonment with his energies intact. Even more remarkable was that he showed no bitterness or desire for revenge.

Despite the oppression of South Africa's black population, Nelson Mandela had been able to become a lawyer. Beginning in the 1940s, he became involved in the ANC—African National Congress—which fought for equal conditions for the different peoples of South Africa.

Apartheid, South Africa's policy of the separation of races, became increasingly more strict. At the beginning of the 1960s, the struggle against apartheid became more heated. Mandela was one of those who held that the principle of protest without violence was no longer worth maintaining, and participated in the organization of an armed struggle.

Mandela lived on the run from the police. In 1962, he was arrested, and later was sentenced to life in prison. During his imprisonment, he refused to make petitions or retract his opinions to win his freedom, and instead stood fast on his demands for freedom for all the peoples of South Africa. The time in prison never made him bitter or hateful. Instead, his views developed in another direction:

"It was during those long and lonely years that my hunger for the freedom of my own people became a hunger for the freedom of all people, white and black. I knew as well as I knew anything that the oppressor must

As a young man Nelson Mandela was a skilled boxer.

< Mandela sewing clothes in prison in Pretoria before being sent to the prison on Robben Island.

be liberated just as surely as the oppressed. A man who takes away another man's freedom is a prisoner of hatred, he is locked behind the bars of prejudice and narrow-mindedness."

Mandela's self-control and farsightedness was a strong contributing factor in the relatively bloodless nature of the great revolution in South African society. Some wondered how Mandela could accept the Nobel Peace Prize, since he had to share it with F.W. de Klerk, whom he had criticized so severely. Mandela replied that earlier conflicts must not be allowed to disturb the negotiation process. "To make peace with an enemy one must work with that enemy, and that enemy becomes one's partner."
o Nelson Mandela, Nobel Peace Prize, 1993.

A Bible and a pair of glasses helped Kim Dae-jung through his time in prison.

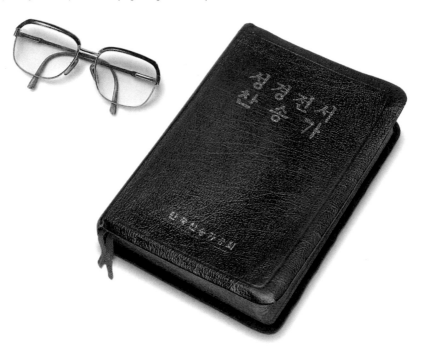

Patient opposition

Kim Dae-jung

Kim Dae-jung has spent most of his political life in opposition. Although he has been thwarted and persecuted in his struggle against authoritarian regimes, he has never lost his faith that everything could ultimately work out for the good.

An important part of Kim Dae-jung's long campaign for peace and freedom has been devoted to reestablishing relations between North and South Korea. After years of control by Japan, Korea was divided into two states following the end of WWII. A few years later war broke out between North Korea and China on one side and South Korea, the United Nations and the United States on the other. The war ended in 1953 with the signing of a cease-fire agreement, but relations between the two nations remained strained.

During the Korean War, Kim Dae-jung was able to escape from Communist imprisonment. Since that time, he has fought for freedom and democracy. During the 1960s, he was elected to several terms in South Korea's National Assembly. After nearly winning the presidential election in 1971, he entered a period of great difficulty. He spent long periods in prison and under house arrest, and attempts were made on his life. In 1981 he was sentenced to death for alleged subversive activities. Following international pressure, the death sentence was reduced to life imprisonment. Eventually, Kim was released from prison and spent a period in exile.

In 1997 Kim Dae-jung was elected president of South Korea. One of his goals has been the reunification of South and North Korea by peaceful means. In 2000, he became the first South Korean leader to visit North

Kim Dae-jung and Kim Jong-il hold hands prior to signing the "June 14 South-North Joint Declaration," Pyongyang in 2000.

Korea. Most recently an improvement in relations between the two countries has occurred. However, Kim Dae-jung has been cautious about awakening hopes of a quick and simple reunification. Reaching the goal may require many more years of work.

Kim Dae-jung has broad interests. During his imprisonment he read great quantities of books on various topics, including philosophy, politics, economics, history, and theology. In his Christian faith he found the strength to endure his tribulations. Kim Dae-jung's involvement in the cause of peace has gone far beyond the issue of the reunification of the two nations of the Korean Peninsula. The broad scope of his interests is reflected in his efforts to promote exchanges between countries and cultures. His struggle for peace, justice, and prosperity applies to all nations on earth.

o Kim Dae-jung, Nobel Peace Prize, 2000.

Kim Dae-jung at presidential rally in November 1970 at Hyochang Stadium, Seoul. In the election race against president Park Chung-hee the following year, Kim lost by a small number of votes.

Kim Dae-jung holding a press conference in Seoul, after being rescued from kidnapping by secret agents in Tokyo, August 1973.

When Kim Dae-jung was taken to the University hospital by force in 1978, he wrote letters by scratching with a nail on food wrappers. The pieces of paper were smuggled out of prison.

After being sentenced to death in 1981, Kim Dae-jung was sent to the Chungju prison. Visits by the family were restricted. Kim's wife, Lee Hee-ho, knitted clothes and blankets that would provide more warmth than the prison uniform.

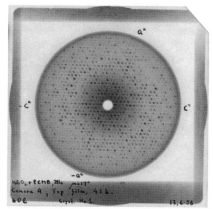

The Buerger Precession Camera. In the early 1940s, M. J. Buerger, a professor of mineralogy at the Massachusetts Institute of Technology, invented an ingenious new x-ray camera. On its x-ray diffraction photographs, such as the one shown here, the spots are arranged at the corners of a three-dimensional lattice that is the reciprocal of the real lattice. These photographs were more straightforward to interpret than the ones taken with other types of cameras used before.

The precession camera moves the crystal about one of its axes like a spinning top. Perutz and Kendrew used it together with a home-built x-ray tube with a rotating anode that produced a beam ten times more intense than any commercial tube. Thanks to these instruments, they were better equipped for protein crystallography than any other laboratory in the world; this contributed decisively to their solution of the first protein structures.

Hard work's reward

Max Perutz

Max Perutz's quest to discover the structure of hemoglobin required the collection of huge amounts of data, gigantic calculations, and relentless analysis. Hemoglobin is the compound that allows the blood to transport energy-giving oxygen to the muscles. Perutz believed that it is not fully possible to understand the functions of a compound unless one knew its molecular structure. With this belief in mind, he began his studies of hemoglobin.

His studies were made possible through the use of x-ray crystallography. In this procedure, a crystal of the compound to be analyzed is bombarded with x-rays, which are captured on a photographic plate. The result is a photographic silhouette of the crystal's molecules. By taking such photographs from many angles, it is possible to build up a three-dimensional image of the molecular structure of the compound. Hemoglobin molecules are extremely large and intricate, and the work to chart out their structure was incredibly painstaking.

It took Perutz six years to gather data in the form of x-ray photographs. After that, he could begin what he called "the real work." Each of the photographs were interpreted through lengthy mathematical operations. Computer technology was still in its infancy, but Perutz was able to conduct his calculations with the help of punch card computers. He was gradually able to build up maps of the molecules, which when laid one over the other gave a three-dimensional image.

The biblical story of Joseph tells of "seven lean years." Perutz said that his research had gone through sixteen lean years of rather boring, routine laboratory work. These years were not without their disappointments. At

Max Perutz with his model of hemoglobin and John Kendrew with his model of myoglobin.

one point, Perutz believed he had developed a successful model. However, one of his students, future Nobel Prize recipient Francis Crick, was able to determine that the model was faulty. In the belief that seven years' research had come to nothing, Perutz was overcome by despair.

After much continued work, Perutz and his colleagues finally did discover the structure of the hemoglobin molecule. In his younger days, Perutz had been an avid mountain climber. He said that the feelings of happiness he felt at his scientific victory were "like reaching the top of a mountain after a very hard climb and falling in love at the same time."

o Max Perutz, Nobel Prize in Chemistry, 1962.

Bror Strandberg and Richard Dickerson outside the hub with the output from the electronic digital computer Edsac II. The pictured tapes specified the phases of the x-ray reflections used to calculate the first atomic model of a protein: sperm whale myoglobin.

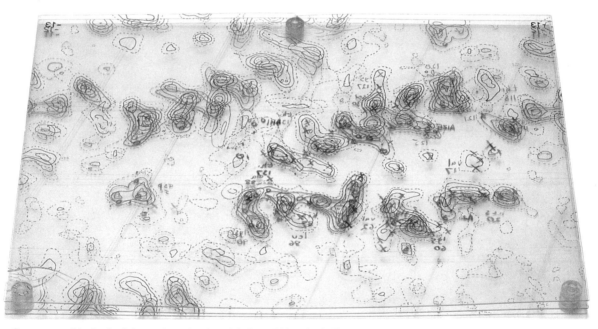

Contour maps of the density of electrons in sections through the hemoglobin molecule. The maps show clearly that the protein chains form helices, and the shapes of the branches extending from the helices allow one to identify the different amino acids, provided their sequence has been chemically determined. The maps were calculated from the x-ray diffraction photographs. The maps formed the basis for the construction of the atomic model.

Model of the hemoglobin moelcule. In total, the molecule consists of around ten thousand atoms. In this model each ball represents an amino acid. The molecule consists of four chains of amino acids. There is one heme group associated with each chain. The heme groups are represented by pink balls in the model. At the heme groups, clefts are formed. These clefts enable the hemoglobin in the blood to transport the energizing oxygen to the muscles of the body.

Max Perutz showing his model of hemoglobin.

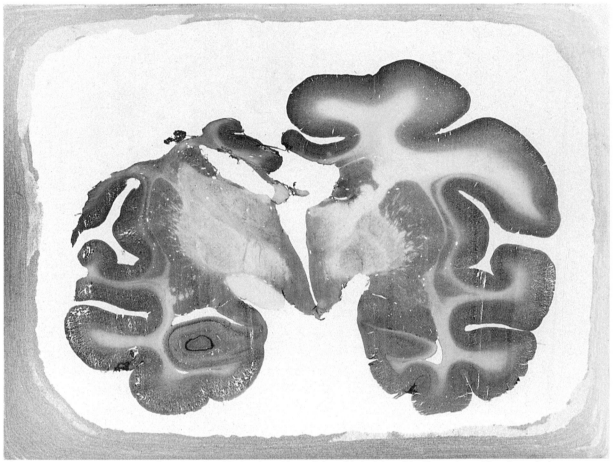

Cross-section of a monkey brain. Roger Sperry's studies of the functions of the two halves of the brain has elicited interest beyond the spheres of science. How is human thought and creativity ordered and structured? How does the capacity for analysis and logical thinking relate to spatial comprehension and the ability to see things in their entirety?

The split brain

Roger Sperry

"Use the right side of your brain!" Have you ever heard this when creative thinking was needed? The greatest advances in our understanding of how the two halves of the brain differ in their functions were made by neurologist Roger Sperry. Sperry spent years systematically examining changes in behavior that occur in both animals and people when the two hemispheres of the brain can no longer communicate with one another.

The connections between the two hemispheres of the brain may be cut off due to injury or surgical procedures. Some people who suffer from a certain type of epilepsy may have to have such surgery. In such cases, the effects on the person's general behavior are surprisingly small. People and animals can usually function quite normally in their everyday lives even when the connections between the halves of the brain have been severed.

It had been known for many years that each side of the brain controls the opposite side of the body, i.e., the left hemisphere controls the right hand, etc. The split-brain research done by Sperry and his colleagues showed that the two halves function almost as two separate brains. If one side of the brain is injured in some way, the other half may be trained to take over its functions as well.

Sperry's split-brain research leads to some interesting questions about human consciousness. What is the relationship between the brain and consciousness? Sperry held that consciousness was not a one-way relationship whereby the brain creates consciousness, but rather an exchange; consciousness also helps to determine the functions of the brain.

In general, the left brain is used for analytical and

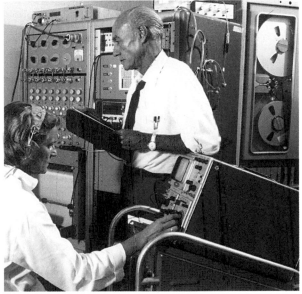
Roger Sperry in his laboratory.

sequential thinking and language, while the right brain is used for intuitive thinking, parallel thought processes, and spatial understanding. Some interpretations of the different functions of the two brains propose that creativity originates in the intuitive functions of the right brain. At times, this idea on the nature of creativity has been overemphasized. Sperry's research does not lend it much support, and his own patient work shows that even faulty assumptions may be useful in making groundbreaking discoveries.

o Roger Sperry, Nobel Prize in Physiology or Medicine, 1981.

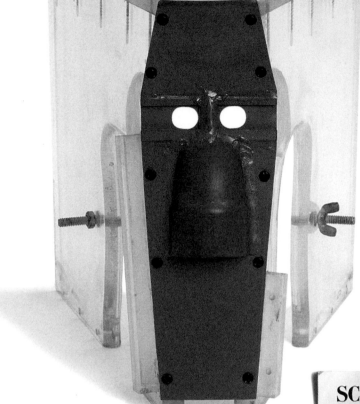

In this box, monkeys with their brain hemispheres cut off from each other could be studied. By closing the little opening for one of the eyes, the hemispheres could be studied separately.

Scalpels and other equipment of Roger Sperry.

740 Russian refugees arrive in Novorossijsk on the Black Sea on the January 10, 1923.

Nansen visiting the Soviet Union in connection with the relief work in 1922.

The Nansen passports gave many refugees a possibility of leaving their camps.

Will and convictions

Fridtjof Nansen

Unbending will, strength, and energy characterize Fridtjof Nansen's efforts in the cause of peace. In the so-called "Nansen passports," his hard work and good ideas took on a tangible form.

Fridtjof Nansen is best known as an explorer, but he devoted the later portion of his life to diplomatic and humanitarian activities, and served as a delegate to the League of Nations.

After WWI, entire regions of Europe and Asia lay in ruins, and chaotic conditions were rampant. Nearly a half a million people waited to return to their homes. The majority of these were Russians who had been prisoner during the conflicts between Germany and Russia.

Russian student volunteers carry provisions being transported to the needy in Saratov in 1921. Nansen is at the left.

Starving, sick, and homeless, they were unwelcome in the places where they now found themselves, but were unable to obtain passports in order to travel home.

The League of Nations assigned Nansen the task of finding a solution to the refugee problem. With unflagging energy, he traveled widely to negotiate with various parties. He was able to generate interest for his plan to issue special passports. These "Nansen passports" won wide international recognition, and gave many people the chance to find their way home. Nansen's work also resulted in an international refugee office, the Nansen Bureau.

One of Nansen's greatest efforts was directed against hunger in Russia. Between 20 and 30 million people were at risk of starvation. Transport problems, lack of funding, and political entanglements made any solution difficult. Some of those able to help were distrustful, and wondered if aid would reach those it was intended for, but Nansen succeeded in convincing all sides involved. Although several million died of starvation, tens of millions more survived, in great part thanks to the aid efforts.

Nansen was already well known as an explorer and researcher when he made his greatest humanitarian contributions. His broad, groundbreaking activity and his stubborn, ingenious work make him an archetype of the creative individual.

o Fridtjof Nansen, Nobel Peace Prize, 1922.

One of August Krogh's inventions was a so-called microclimato-graph, which he designed in 1938–1939. The microclimatograph was carried between the clothes and the body and registered temperature and humidity. The temperature was measured by a spiral of bimetal and the humidity by a hair. These measuring devices were connected to a small needle that left tracks on a smoked disc. The disc was rotated by a clock-work, allowing the changes in temperature and humidity to be registered.

A young August Krogh in his study.

Krogh at an experimental set-up.

Bedtime thoughts

August Krogh

Working in bed—can it be effective? Physiologist August Krogh thought so. He described what he referred to as his "visual thinking":

"I did a considerable part of my work while I lay in bed in the evening. There I tried to imagine the processes which I should try to understand and the experiments I should perform. I found that I could see quite complicated arrangements before me, with all the details of their functions. My fruitful ideas came seemingly out of the blue, but the way in which I worked through them in my thoughts was a conscious, rational process. I never made sketches, and I do not to this day, not even rough sketches, not before I had completed the arrangement in my thoughts, since I felt that a sketch would hinder my ideas from flowing freely, and limit me to a certain solution of the problem."

The ability to see things even when they exist only in the mind is an important resource for creative work. August Krogh's capacity for constructive thought became evident early on. He greedily devoured books about technology and science and reconstructed the experiments they described. When he eventually entered the field of science himself, it was clear that he had a natural tendency toward hard work. He constructed all the equipment for his experiments by himself. His plans for his experiments were simple and straightforward, but his equipment was often so ingenious that only Krogh himself could operate it.

Krogh's work stretched across several disciplines. At an early point he developed methods for precision measurement of the gas content of liquids, including for exam-

August and Marie Krogh shared their interest in science.

ple oxygen levels in the blood. The work for which he was awarded a Nobel Prize dealt with how the body regulates the supply of oxygen to the muscles during work. Previously, it was believed that the speed of blood circulation was increased during physical exertion. However, Krogh proved that the body actually regulated oxygen supply by the opening of more capillaries, the smallest blood vessels. During rest, relatively few capillaries are open.

Krogh's varied research took up most of his time. Didn't his habit of working constantly, including while he lay in bed, wear him out? August Krogh's career was actually like play to him, and he never felt pressured by it. A happy circumstance that probably eased his home life was that his wife Marie was also his colleague. In their marriage the two shared a common interest in scientific problems.

o August Krogh, Nobel Prize in Physiology or Medicine, 1920.

A wobbling plate from Cornell University had an important influence on the physical theories of Richard Feynman.

Inspiration from play

Richard Feynman

Probably the most playful of all Nobel Prize recipients was Richard Feynman. Playful curiosity characterized Feynman's scientific work, as well as the rest of his life.

During WWII, Feynman was a member of the Manhattan Project, the research group that developed the atomic bomb. After the war ended, he returned to the academic world. Although he was a successful teacher, Feynman made little progress in his research. He tried and tried, but seemed to get nowhere. Feelings of discontentment overtook him, and he began to analyze the successes of his past. He realized then that his playful attitude toward theories and constructions were what had driven his research.

One day in the university cafeteria, he watched someone toss a spinning dinner plate into the air. As the plate

Richard Feynman enjoyed playing the bongo drums as well as juggling.

spun, it wobbled. Feynman was prompted to formulate these motions as a problem in equations, which he could then analyze. Soon he found himself working with other physics problems by using similar techniques and everyday observations. He had rediscovered happiness and inspiration in his work.

Feynman's research centered around finding a fundamental theory of how electromagnetic radiation such as light interacts with atoms. He sought to unite electrodynamics and quantum mechanics. Throughout the 1930s, physicists had studied numerous questions connected with these problems. Following WWII, new disoveries were made possible by advances in technology. Thanks to his earlier experiences, it was Feynman who found a method of performing calculations that clarified these new discoveries. After discussions with his colleagues, he was eventually able to formulate his theory of quantum electrodynamics.

Feynman's theory involves much more than just his own ideas or the single insight he gained in that moment in the university cafeteria. Nonetheless, it was that moment of light-hearted observation that inspired his research. Feynman wrote that "It was effortless. It was easy to play with these things. I almost tried to resist it! There was no importance to what I was doing, but ultimately there was. The diagrams and the whole business that I got the Nobel Prize for came from that piddling around with the wobbling plate."

o Richard Feynman, Nobel Prize in Physics, 1965.

Relief from demands
Rabindranath Tagore

Sometimes rather ordinary things can help release creative powers. Rabindranath Tagore used a simple slate as a tool for releasing his creative powers. He told of the great relief he felt when he began to write on a slate instead of in a manuscript book. The manuscript books demanded that he fill them with something valuable. The slate freed him from these demands, since everything could be erased in one stroke.

Tagore felt that the poetic style that had been forced upon him limited his creativity. During a period of time spent alone, isolated from people he felt obligated to please, he found a way out of his rut. One morning inspiration came bubbling forth. Tagore stood on his veranda and watched as the sun rose between the treetops:

"As I gazed, all of a sudden a lid seemed to fall from my eyes, and I found the world bathed in a wonderful radiance, with waves of beauty and joy swelling on every side. The radiance pierced the folds of sadness and despondency which had accumulated over my heart, and flooded it with universal light.

That very day the poem 'Nirjharer Swapnabhanga' (The Fountain's Awakening) gushed forth and coursed in like a cascade. The poem ended, but the curtain did not fall upon my joy."

Tagore describes inspiration resembling a religious experience, almost like a feeling of salvation.

Western readers often find the religious and mystical to be the most prevalent elements of Tagore's poetry. With his long beard and hair, and clothed in robes, he did seem the archetypal Eastern mystic. In India and

< Self-portrait by Rabindranath Tagore.

Presentday slate from Rabindranath Tagore's Bengal.

Bangladesh, however, Tagore was seen as a relevant and multifaceted thinker who expressed his ideas regarding culture, society, and politics in practical, everyday terms. Tagore stood for sound reasoning, the freedom of thought, and cultural diversity. He preferred critical scientific methods over traditions not founded upon reason.

Tagore was indeed a many-faceted figure able to deal with the worldly as well as the deeply spiritual. His long life of creativity encompassed poetry, the visual arts, politics, philosophy, and religion.

o Rabindranath Tagore, Nobel Prize in Literature, 1913.

Tagore and Gandhi. Early on, Tagore engaged himself in the search for a new Indian consciousness, and participated in the opposition against British colonialism. It was Tagore who gave Gandhi the title Mahatma ("Great Soul"), and next to Gandhi, he was a symbol of the new India. Despite their mutual respect for one another, the two were frequently at odds. Tagore felt that Gandhi lost himself in meaningless symbolic acts.

Rabindranath and Abanindranath Tagore.

Tagore painting.

The moment of inspiration

Selma Lagerlöf

A pair of Selma Lagerlöf's shoes reveals her limping gait by their heels of different heights. Lagerlöf's physical challenge meant that some of life's choices were more accessible to her than others. She claimed that this was one of the main reasons that she became a teacher and author, rather than a housewife and mother.

Curiously enough, the inspiration for her monumental debut novel *Gösta Berling's Saga* came to her while she was walking. In a fairy tale-like short story entitled "The Tale of a Tale," she tells of how her creative powers as an author were awakened. The stories that had surrounded her during her childhood and youth in the Swedish province of Värmland seized her imagination one day.

She was twenty-two years old, and was in Stockholm, studying to be a teacher. Most of her time was taken up by studies instead of writing. One day, as she walked home from a lecture in literary history, she thought about the great Swedish-language poets Bellman and Runeberg and the characters presented in their works. She was struck by the insight that the stories and characters she had known as a girl could be just as fantastic.

"And thus it was that she first caught a glimpse of the tale. And when she saw it, the ground beneath her feet began to sway. The street she was walking upon, Malmskillnadsgatan, swayed along its entire length, from the hill at Hamngatan all the way up to the fire station. It heaved toward the sky and sank down again, heaved and sank. She had to stand still for a good while before it stopped moving. She looked in amazement as others walked calmly by, without noticing the amazing thing that had just come to pass.

In this moment, the young girl decided that she would write about the cavaliers of Värmland. She never gave up this thought, but many years would go by before her decision came to fruition."

Many authors seem to have had this type of experience. It is a great discovery to find that the tale that must be told is right under one's nose, and that the stories one thought were worthless are worth telling—one only needs to learn how to tell them.
o Selma Lagerlöf, Nobel Prize in Literature, 1909.

Selma Lagerlöf as a young woman.

The context of insight

Charles Townes

Early one morning in April 1951, physicist Charles H. Townes sat down on a park bench in Washington, DC. He was in town for a meeting with a committee working to develop the technology of short wave radiation, also known as microwaves. Since he was the committee chair, Townes wanted to think some things over before the meeting. He was especially interested in the radiation that results from transitions of electrons from a higher to a lower energy level. He suddenly had an idea that it ought to be possible to construct a sort of resonator that could reflect this radiation back into the molecular structure, thereby setting up a resonance that would produce intense radiation on a constant wavelength.

Townes' idea became the basis for the development of the maser. Eventually the same principle was used in the development of the laser, which uses light rather than microwaves.

This story is a typical example of how a single moment of insight may lead to a significant development. Yet Townes' story is also one of university research backed by military financing.

After WWII, the U.S. government invested huge amounts of money in the research and development of strategic military technologies. One such field was electronics. The influx of government funding led to the expansion of electronics facilities at a number of U.S. universities. In his daily life, Townes was employed at Columbia University's radiation laboratory, which in the 1950s had one of the best programs for microwave research. Microwaves were of interest to the military because they could be generated by a relatively small, compact apparatus. This meant that they had potential uses in weapons systems such as missiles, tanks, and submarine periscopes. The government research committee that Townes headed had been formed by the U.S. Navy to identify promising areas of research for funding.

The individual components of Townes' idea were not new. It had been known for decades that molecules could be made to emanate radiation of constant wavelength, and electronics engineers had been using systems of amplification for years. Townes was accomplished in both molecular spectroscopy and radar electronics. He was thus especially well qualified to combine these two technologies—and his work on the microwave committee created the opportunity for him to do so.

○ Charles Townes, Nobel Prize in Physics, 1964.

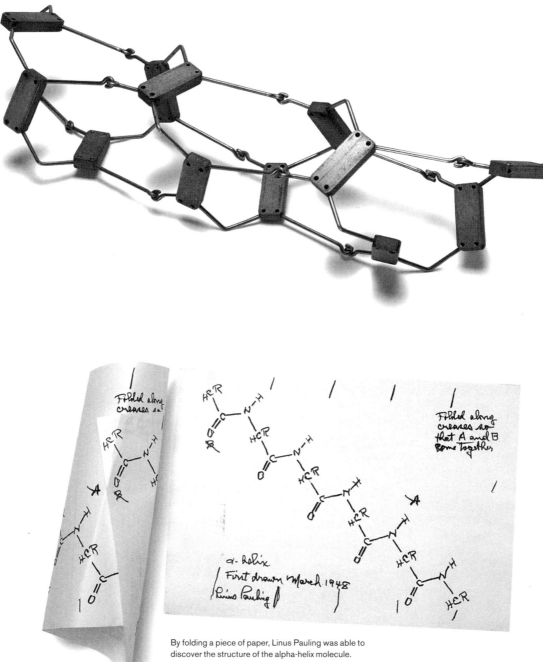

By folding a piece of paper, Linus Pauling was able to
discover the structure of the alpha-helix molecule.

Train your subconscious mind!

Linus Pauling

Linus Pauling often thought about scientific questions just before he fell asleep at night, in hopes that his subconscious mind would work on them while he slept or at other times even when he was not actively working. After a long dormancy, a question could suddenly be reactivated, and the solution could hit Pauling in the form of a sudden instinct.

"Hunches, or inspirations, come to me often when I have thought about a problem for years and then have suddenly found an answer. This is because I train my subconscious mind to retain and ponder problems . . ."

Pauling exemplified this process in the story of his work with alpha keratin molecules. The components of keratin, a material found in hair, were well known, but the appearance of its molecules was unknown. In 1937, Pauling devoted his efforts to discovering this structure. He believed the molecule consisted of a long string of connected atoms, which he called a polypeptide chain. But the precise arrangement of the atoms into a molecule remained a mystery that Pauling worked on for several years, without results.

Then in 1948, Pauling went to Oxford to spend several semesters there. In April, he came down with a heavy cold that confined him to bed. He began reading novels, but soon became bored, and decided instead to attack his old problem. Still believing that the polypeptide chain was the basis of the keratin molecule, he took a piece of paper and sketched how he imagined the molecule would look if it were laid out flat. He then tried to fold the paper at the points where the molecular structure would allow it. After several attempts, he succeeded in folding the paper

Linus Pauling absorbed in thought on the couch in his office.

to form a pipe-like formation that would allow the molecular structure to hook into itself and thus form a spiral. All of the pieces of Pauling's puzzle had suddenly fallen into place.

The alpha-helix molecule, as it came to be called, was an important discovery. However, it was only one of many during Pauling's broad and varied career. Many of his contributions have provided the very foundation of modern chemistry: the knowledge of how atoms bind to one another and form molecules. The discovery of the alpha-helix molecule illustrates one of Linus Pauling's great talents—the capacity to think visually.

o Linus Pauling, Nobel Prize in Chemistry, 1954.

Ava Helen and Linus Pauling shared not only their commitment to peace but also some parts of his scientific work. The model above was built by them in the 1930s and represents the structure for the mineral zunyite, one of the structures Linus Pauling discovered.

The rush of creativity

Erwin Schrödinger

Waves, waves! Everything comes in waves!

Quantum theory rocked the world view of classical physics, and in the end supplanted it. One of the most decisive steps toward this new world view was achieved by Erwin Schrödinger. During a period of intense, boiling creativity he formulated his theory of wave mechanics, as well as other groundbreaking ideas.

While Niels Bohr's atomic model was a functional, semi-classical theory for quantum atomic phenomena, it proved to be incomplete. A number of physicists, Erwin Schrödinger among them, began the search for a comprehensive theory that could explain more of the quantum effects observable in the microcosmos. Yet following his appointment as a professor at the University of Zurich in 1921, Schrödinger's time was consumed by teaching and other practical demands, forcing him to set his research aside. Finally, in autumn 1925, Schrödinger found the piece of the puzzle that he needed while reading Louis de Broglie's doctoral dissertation, published that year. De Broglie proposed that quantum phenomena might be traceable to wave motion associated with the electron paths of an atom. Schrödinger's mind was jarred into action. During the 1925–1926 Christmas vacation, he formulated the first version of his theory of wave mechanics, which illustrates quantum phenomena in terms of intrinsic values. During the coming months, Schrödinger wrote four papers that became the foundation of the study of quantum mechanics.

Schrödinger's private life was less than peaceful, and

Erwin Schrödinger lecturing.

this period of intense creativity coincided with an especially stormy time in his marriage. And he was not in the habit of sacrificing his free time to his work. Upon his return to Zurich after the Christmas vacation, he was asked if he had enjoyed the skiing. He answered that he had been distracted by "some calculations." It has been said that this was the only time in his life that Schrödinger allowed anything to disturb his vacation.

Since Schrödinger needed absolute silence in order to work, he sometimes used pearls as earplugs—a trick he resorted to often during the spring of 1926.

o Erwin Schrödinger, Nobel Prize in Physics, 1933.

< Schrödinger among the waves and a page in a notebook where he wrote down the thoughts that led to the wave equation.

The Battle of Solferino, painted by Carlo Bossoli. When Henry Dunant witnessed the battle, his life was changed. He devoted all his powers to the struggle for peace and founded the Red Cross.

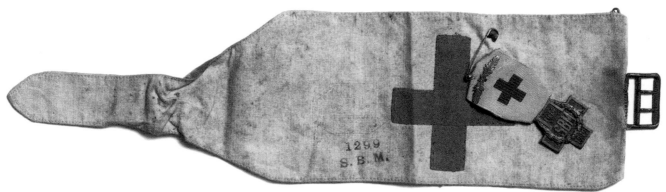

Sleeve badge from WW I. The sleeve badge with a red cross on a white background became the distinctive mark for the Red Cross personnel.

An unintentional consequence

Henry Dunant

In the spring of 1859, a young Swiss named Henry Dunant arrived in Paris, determined to gain an audience with Emperor Napoleon III. Dunant had a brilliant idea for the cultivation of a tract of land he had purchased in Algeria. He needed permission from the emperor to obtain water from the surrounding lands, which were owned by the French government. Unfortunately, Napoleon was in Italy with his troops, waging war against the Austrian army.

Dunant set off for Italy to find the emperor. His search

brought him to the scene of the Battle of Solferino. The battle claimed 40,000 lives in one day. Many of the injured soldiers who might have survived died due to lack of water on the parched, scorching battlefield. The terrible human suffering Dunant saw at Solferino changed his life.

In the account he wrote of his experiences, *A Memory of Solferino*, Dunant suggested the establishment of an international volunteer organization that would care for wounded soldiers. Dunant disseminated his book to governments and influential people throughout Europe, and began an energetic fight for the cause of peace. Due to his efforts, the International Red Cross was established in 1863. At the Geneva Convention of 1864, many nations guaranteed that the Red Cross would be allowed to assist wounded soldiers in time of war. An armband with a red cross on a white background became the emblem of the Red Cross volunteers.

Dunant became known around the world, and was involved in many issues of the day. However, his lack of attention to his own personal affairs resulted in deep financial difficulties. In later years, he lived forgotten and poor in a tiny village. A journalist who discovered him there published an interview with him. The world was surprised to hear that the famous Dunant was still alive, and soon he began to receive awards and monetary contributions. As the culmination of this new attention, Dunant was awarded the Nobel Peace Prize. Dunant's fight for peace continued. For the rest of his life he lived simply, and left most of his money to charitable causes.
o Henry Dunant, Nobel Peace Prize, 1901.

The dish in which Alexander Fleming's culture was attacked by mold.
The discovery led to the development of penicillin.

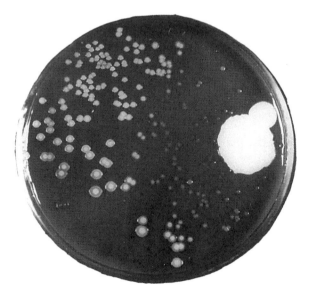

Chance as method

Alexander Fleming

One day in the summer of 1928, Alexander Fleming picked up a leftover culture dish in which he had grown bacteria. He saw that mold had also begun to grow in the dish. While there was nothing unusual about that, Fleming did notice something remarkable. The mold seemed to be preventing spread of the bacteria in the petridish. The discovery led to the development of penicillin.

Exactly how Fleming discovered penicillin remains in dispute. In any case, what is known is that spores from the mold had drifted into Fleming's laboratory and had gained a foothold in the leftover culture dish. Fleming's discovery cannot be seen as a pure coincidence, since he routinely left used bacteria samples standing, in order to observe what would happen to them. Fleming often said that he never would have made any discoveries if his laboratory had been clean and orderly.

Although Fleming discovered penicillin, he never participated in the developmental work that made it possible to produce penicillin commercially. That work was undertaken ten years later by Howard Florey and Ernst Boris Chain and their colleagues. Why didn't Fleming persevere in the development of penicillin himself? One answer is that Fleming's research focused on finding agents that would stimulate the body's immune defense, i.e., vaccines, rather than medicines that would attack bacteria. Another answer is that such work was not part of Fleming's personality. His strength was as a leisurely discoverer rather than as a methodical, long-term worker. Yet another answer is that Fleming mostly worked alone – the development of penicillin required a multi-dicipli-nary team of researches.

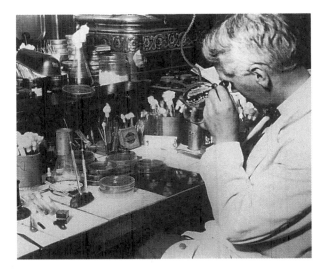

Fleming was not a fanatical, devoted researcher, and his work days were not unusually long. In the afternoons, he went to the Chelsea Arts Club for afternoon tea, to play billiards or cards, have a drink, and then go home to his family for dinner at eight o'clock in the evening. He spent his weekends in the country, took long vacations, and had many interests outside his work. For Fleming, scientific research was not a great, all-consuming calling.

When the newspapers began to report on the discovery of penicillin in 1942, it was Fleming who reaped the honors. Yet Fleming remained as reserved and humble as ever, and seemed unconcerned about personal gain or success.

o Alexander Fleming, Nobel Prize in Physiology or Medicine, 1945.

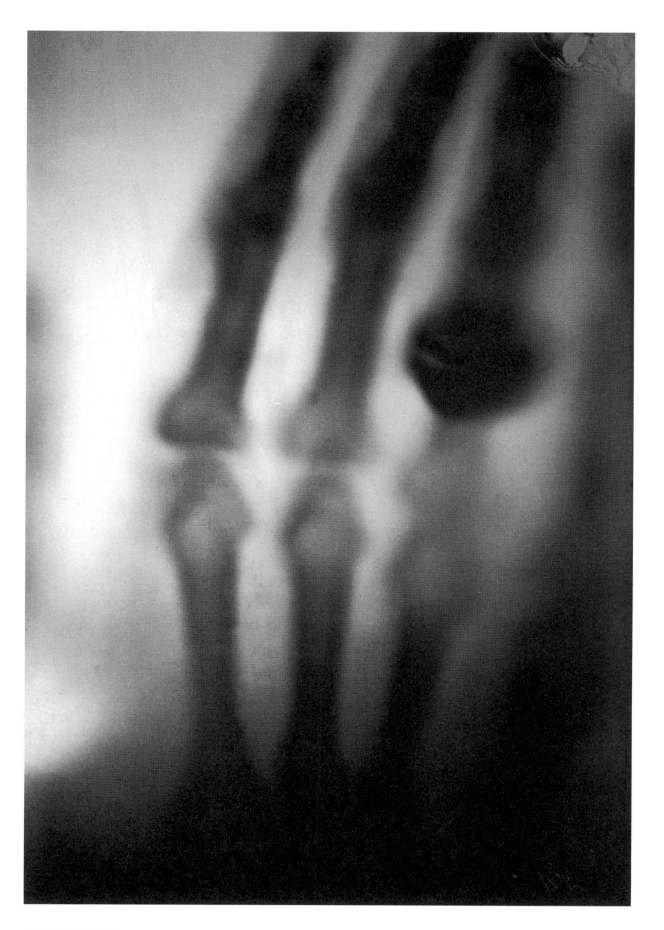

The interpretation of the unexpected

Wilhelm Röntgen

Chance may often be the basis for a major discovery, but successfully interpreting a chance discovery usually requires huge amounts of work.

On November 8, 1895, physicist Wilhelm Röntgen stood in his laboratory. He was busily researching cathode rays, which are produced when an electric current is run between two metal plates that are held inside a glass vacuum tube. Some of the cathode rays stream out of the tube through a tiny window of clear glass. The rays are visible when they shine on plates of light-sensitive material, and can only shine as far as eight centimeters away from the glass tube.

To prevent light disturbances, Röntgen had shrouded his work space in black crepe, and extinguished all lights in the room. By chance, he had left one plate of light-sensitive material on a chair several meters away from the cathode ray tube. After his eyes had become accustomed to the darkness, Röntgen noticed something very strange. On the plate on the chair, he could see a faint light. If the plate had been standing up to eight centimeters from the tube, he would have seen exactly what he expected to. This new light phenomenon at first seemed unexplainable. It seemed to be able to pass through solid materials! Röntgen stopped his work on his original experiment, and devoted himself to finding out more about the newly discovered phenomenon. He decided not to tell anyone about his discovery, and spent seven weeks alone in his laboratory studying the new rays.

After an intensive period of making examinations,

Röntgen decided to publish an article on his findings. The capability of this new radiation to shine through different materials with different intensities provided new opportunities for seeing things that previously had been hidden. Potential applications for its uses soon became evident, not the least of which were in the field of medicine.

After his discovery, Röntgen became famous. However, he soon lost his interest in x-rays, and after 1897, he conducted no further experiments on them.
o Wilhelm Röntgen, Nobel Prize in Physics, 1901.

< Wilhelm Röntgen's picture of the hand of his wife Bertha, in which the skeleton and the wedding ring could be seen, quickly became famous.

In 1909 a concerned chicken farmer brought this hen to the Rockefeller Institute. The hen's tumor was the origin of the research that led to Peyton Rous's discovery of a virus that causes cancer. Recognition of the discovery took a long time. Rous was 31 years old when he published his discovery in 1911 and had reached age 87 when he was finally awarded the Nobel Prize in 1966.

Making your own chances

Peyton Rous

"Chance favors the prepared mind," the famous scientist Louis Pasteur once said. Pathologist Peyton Rous spoke instead of "a prepared mind making its own chances."

Soon after being appointed head of cancer research at the Rockefeller Institute in New York in 1909, the young Rous was visited by a chicken farmer. The farmer wanted help with a prize-winning chicken that had a tumor. Here Rous saw an opportunity to test his theory that cancer was caused by a virus. When he injected a filtered, cell-free sample of the tumor into healthy chickens, they developed cancerous growths. Rous concluded that tumor cells release a transmitting agent, a virus, that causes cancer.

The discovery was both upsetting and important, and Rous's experiment was initially received with interest. However, the continuation of the story proved to be more complicated and mysterious. When no one, not even Rous himself, was able to reproduce the same results in mammals, contemporary researchers dismissed the discovery as irrelevant to the further understanding of cancer. Rous left cancer research in 1915, and for the next twenty years directed his attention toward other areas. In the mid 1930s he resumed his research on cancer, albeit with a different focus.

Peyton Rous lived a long life filled with patient, habitual work. He began and ended his workday by writing. The middle of his day was devoted to several hours of intense discussions with colleagues in the Institute's cafeteria, and afternoons were spent in the laboratory with his experiments.

Although Rous's days were marked by routine, the sto-

Rous at his microscope.

ry of his most famous discovery, the chicken virus, shows how research may take an unexpected turn. Even after Rous's death, the story of the chicken virus has continued to prove this point. Science has shown that viruses take effect by invading the genes of normal cells. In the 1970s, researchers continuing the study of Rous's chicken virus successfully isolated the gene that causes cancer. Thus a chicken tumor from the beginning of the century took a central role in the search for the cause of cancer.

○ Peyton Rous, Nobel Prize in Physiology or Medicine, 1966.

Over a long period, Peyton Rous performed research other than the cancer research he started his career with and later received the Nobel Prize for. These flasks were used by Rous in the mid 1930s. It is not exactly clear in which experiment they were used.

Preparation and interpretation

Irène Joliot-Curie and Frédéric Joliot

Often it seems as though great discoveries are placed in the researcher's path by coincidence. Yet unexpected discoveries are often preceded by years of careful preparation and insight that enable the researcher to make the correct interpretation. One such example is Irène Joliot-Curie and Frédéric Joliot's discovery of artificial radioactivity.

Irène Joliot-Curie, the daughter of Marie and Pierre Curie, began working in the same field as her parents. Frédéric Joliot, whom she married in 1926, also worked at the Curies' Radium Institute in Paris. The pair carried out their most important experiment in 1934. It dealt with bombarding an extremely thin layer of aluminum with alpha particles. The layer of aluminum was placed in front of the window of a cloud chamber so that the radiation that occurred when it was bombarded could be studied. However, it was when the bombardment was turned off that an unexpected discovery was made. The aluminum continued to emit radiation! The Joliot-Curies eventually concluded that during the bombardment the aluminum atoms had been transformed into a radioactive isotope of phosphorus. This was the first radioactive atomic nucleus created by artificial means.

The entire experiment required extreme care and a refined technique. The aluminum layer had to be made extremely thin, and the work had to be done within the framework of the three minute half-life of the isotope.

The discovery was a further confirmation that atoms were not the stable, indivisible units scientists had once believed. It was also one of the first steps toward the harnessing of atomic energy, and the creation of the atomic

< Irène and Marie Curie.

Frédéric Joliot and Irène Joliot-Curie.

bomb. Both of the Joliot-Curies continued their research with a focus on uranium fission, the splitting of uranium nuclei. During WWII, however, they wanted to avoid allowing the Germans to gain an advantage from their research. For this reason, their colleagues in fission research moved to England. Frédéric Joliot stayed on in Paris, devoting himself to other research and becoming involved in the resistance movement. Irène and their children spent the war years in Switzerland.

The Joliot-Curies held radical views on social issues. Frédéric Joliot was an avowed communist, and after the war he engaged in the campaign against atomic weapons through various peace organizations. Irène Joliot-Curie, too, was strongly involved in the peace movement, and also worked to improve the position of women in society. ○ Irène Joliot-Curie and Frédéric Joliot, Nobel Prize in Chemistry, 1935.

Joseph Brodsky was once asked to make a drawing showing the role of the muse of inspiration in the creative process. The result was this self-portrait: the poet's *altra ego* stretches out in the Baltic Sea, with the Stockholm City Hall to one side. The text reads "Joseph Brodsky's innermost being." In the open book he has written the opening lines of one of his early poems. The reading cat is Brodsky's variation on the Venetian coat of arms, which depicts the Lion of Saint Mark holding a book in its paw.

An unending exercise in uncertainty

Joseph Brodsky

What is most impressive about a work of art or a scientific discovery? Joseph Brodsky's answer to this question was "the sense of an opened horizon." "'Creativity' is what a vast beach remarks when a grain of sand is swept away by the ocean. If this sounds too tragic or too grand for you, it means only that you are too far back in the dunes."

For Brodsky, creativity was in large part a matter of chance—finding that which is creative at the right point in time. "No amount of research or caffeine, calories, alcohol, or tobacco consumed can position that grain of sand sufficiently close to the breakers. It all depends on the breakers themselves, i.e., on matter's own timing, which is solely responsible for the erosion of its so-called beach."

Creativity seen from within, said Brodsky, is "an unending exercise in uncertainty." The fleeting nature of creativity seemed hard to grasp. He likened these strivings to a cat's attempts to catch its own tail. Brodsky maintained that the only meaningful thing to the one who does something—creative or not—is the work itself. For him, writing was a craving that had to be satisfied:

"The one who writes a poem writes it above all because verse writing is an extraordinary accelerator of conscience, of thinking, of comprehending the universe. Having experienced this acceleration once, one is no longer capable of abandoning the chance to repeat this experience; one falls into dependency on this process, the way others fall into dependency on drugs or on alcohol. One who finds himself in this sort of dependency on language is, I guess, what they call a poet."

Joseph Brodsky had great integrity as a writer and as a human being. He chose his own course against the pre-

Joseph Brodsky photographed by his friend Michail Miltchik at the Leningrad airport immediately before leaving for New York on June 4, 1972.

vailing political system and social conventions. His understanding that a poet required periods of inactivity for the sake of creativity was not appreciated by the Soviet system. He was charged with "social parasitism" and sentenced to hard labor. After being exiled from the Soviet Union in 1972, he moved to New York.

Thus like many other prominent authors, Joseph Brodsky found himself living between two cultures. He sometimes said, "I'm a Russian poet, an English essayist, and an American citizen."

o Joseph Brodsky, Nobel Prize in Literature, 1987.

Mary McDowell and Jane Addams with peace banner around 1930.

Jane Addams at her desk.

U.S. delegation to the International Conference of Women for a Permanent Peace, held at The Hague, Netherlands, 1915. Jane Addams is seated in the front row, second from the left.

Synthesizing experiences

Jane Addams

The name of Jane Addams lives on mainly for her efforts in two areas: social work and the campaign for world peace. There was a connection between her work in the two fields; social work supplied her with ideas that she applied to her work for world peace.

The most famous expression of Addams' social work was Hull House in Chicago. Together with a friend, she rented the building in 1889 as a place in which to establish a center for social work. In the surrounding slums, immigrant groups from many different countries lived in dirty, crowded tenements. Hull House became a place for these people to find recreation and take part in educational activities.

Addams saw how these immigrants from such diverse backgrounds went to great lengths to forge a new sort of community in their adopted homeland. Her experiences inspired her to dream of an international movement for peace. Earlier ideals of peace had been emotionally motivated and "dovelike." Addams felt the time had come for a more proactive and dynamic peace movement. In the immigrant neighborhoods of Chicago, she had seen this new ideal in action.

The outbreak of WWI in 1914 disturbed Addams deeply. In cooperation with representatives from the women's movement, she initiated a conference for various women's organizations. The result of this conference was the Women's Peace Party, with Addams serving as its first chairperson. The new party was duly noted in Europe, and Addams was invited to an international congress at The Hague, Netherlands. The congress made new demands for peace and arbitration, and sent representa-

Jane Addams with children at Hull House in Chicago.

tives to the statesmen of the European countries. Addams herself traveled to London, Berlin, Vienna, Rome, and Paris. The idea of a civil initiative undertaken by laypeople was a new phenomenon in international politics. The delegates were warmly and earnestly received by the world leaders they visited.

Not everyone appreciated Addams' actions, and she had to endure frequent public criticism. Some Americans even saw her work as treacherous. Nonetheless, Jane Addams' work produced lasting results. The international cooperative movements that she began led to the formation of a permanent organization, the Women's International League for Peace and Freedom, where Addams performed a leading role throughout the 1920s.
o Jane Addams, Nobel Peace Prize, 1931.

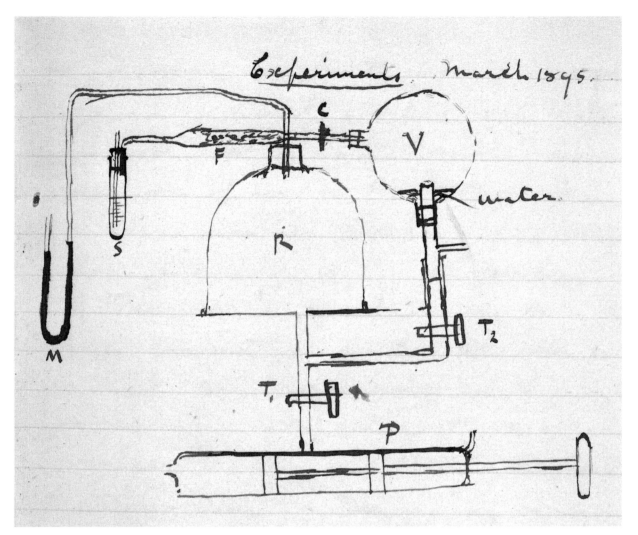

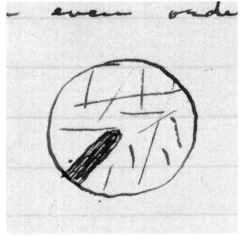

C.T.R Wilson's sketch of his cloud chamber in a notebook from 1895.

In his notebooks, Wilson took notes of what he saw in his cloud chamber. On March 29, 1911, he drew a sketch and wrote: "On one occasion in addition to ordinary thread-like rays, one large finger-like ray was seen, evidently a different form of secondary ray—giving rise to enormously more ionization than even ordinary ray."

An instrument in a new context

C.T.R. Wilson

What causes rain? This was C.T.R. Wilson's question. Wind and weather were Wilson's great scientific interests, but his search for the cause of rain yielded no answers. Instead it led to completely different questions and answers about the smallest units of matter. The "cloud chamber" that Wilson developed was transformed from a tool for the study of weather and light into an instrument for the examination of the basic components of matter.

On his hikes through the Scottish landscape, Wilson became fascinated by different light phenomena that he observed in clouds and fog. In order to study these phenomena more closely, he tried to make artificial fog in a laboratory setting. This was the origin of Wilson's cloud chamber, in which he created clouds in a glass container.

Wilson worked at the Cavendish Laboratory at Cambridge. His colleagues there were studying how electrically charged (or ionized) particles influenced the formation of raindrops. Intrigued by their research, Wilson began to combine his cloud chamber work with experiments on condensation in electromagnetic fields. He continued these experiments for many years. In 1911, he was able to show that electrons left tracks in the cloud chamber, since the ionizing action of the speeding electrons forms droplets. Alpha rays, created by the nuclei of helium atoms, gave similar results. The phenomenon proved very useful: with the help of the cloud chamber, elementary particles were given a visual representation. Measuring the tracks that they left behind revealed their basic characteristics. The world of microphysics had become tangible.

Wilson's greatest contribution to science was the cloud chamber. In the decades that followed, the Cavendish Laboratory embarked upon highly successful research in particle physics, with the cloud chamber as the primary technical aid. Other scientists such as Patrick Blackett further developed the device into an instrument of extreme precision. Wilson continued his own research in atmospheric physics, for which the cloud chamber had little importance. Ionization did not prove to be of significance to the cause of rain. In the end, Wilson's cloud chamber served little use as a tool for understanding atmospheric physics—but as a detector in particle physics, it was a groundbreaking device.

o C.T.R. Wilson, Nobel Prize in Physics, 1927.

Prototype for a control unit for an electrophoresis apparatus, developed by Arne Tiselius.

Combination and transfer

Arne Tiselius

To create something new and unknown from several known phenomena—the act of making a new combination—lies at the heart of creativity. Much of the work of Arne Tiselius had to do with transferring ideas between different disciplines. He conducted his research in the borderlands between chemistry, physics, and biology.

From his mentor Theodore Svedberg, Tiselius gained an interest in the study of large compound molecules

using physical methods. One area that had intrigued Svedberg, but which he had never had time to pursue, was how various materials move through a solution under the influence of an electric current. Svedberg turned this problem over to Tiselius. Since different proteins move through an electric field at different speeds, the method can be used to differentiate between them. The phenomenon, which Tiselius called electrophoresis, provides a useful tool for analyzing the composition of various samples, and is widely used today in biochemical laboratories.

An important creative aspect of Tiselius's research was his role in the development of instruments and apparatuses. Here he had inherited a tradition upon which to build: his teacher Theodore Svedberg made his most important discoveries after he developed the ultramicroscope and the ultracentrifuge. Tiselius's electrophoresis apparatus was a new apparatus in the same tradition of separating different substances from each other.

Tiselius also succeeded in creating an organizational environment that supported progressive research. In his laboratory, he brought together a team of researchers from various disciplines under one roof. While the overcrowded conditions of his institution had obvious disadvantages, they also facilitated fruitful exchange. Tiselius encouraged the brainstorms his students might experience, speaking of "controlled coincidence." These same hopes of cross-disciplinary pollination also inspired Tiselius's noteworthy efforts at scientific cooperation on the international level, for example, with the Rockefeller Institution in the United States.

o Arne Tiselius, Nobel Prize in Chemistry, 1948.

Transplanting an idea

Martin Luther King, Jr.

"I have a dream . . ."

Visionary power has seldom been expressed more clearly than in Martin Luther King's 1963 Washington speech.

As a great leader, King had been inspired by Mahatma Gandhi. He planted the seeds of Gandhi's principle of nonviolent protest in new soil, where they blossomed in a new way.

In 1948 as a young student, King first encountered the ideas of Gandhi. In 1959, he traveled to India. "It was wonderful to be in Gandhi's land," he said upon his return home. "I left India more convinced than ever before that nonviolent resistance is the most potent weapon available to oppressed people in their struggle for freedom."

In his speech at the Nobel Prize ceremonies in 1964, King related how American blacks were following the example of the people of India. They sought to show that nonviolence was not mere passivity, but rather a powerful moral principle that would pave the way for creative social change: "sooner or later all the peoples of the world will have to discover a way to live together in peace, and thereby transform this pending cosmic elegy into a creative psalm of brotherhood."

King stood for peace, but also for resistance. He spoke of the "creative battle" to end injustice. Uncertainty and unrest should not be feared, but should be seen as "the creative turmoil of genuine civilization struggling to be born."

The battle gave results. The U.S. Congress passed sev-

< Martin Luther King, Jr. at his desk under the portrait of Mahatma Gandhi.

eral important laws regarding citizens' rights and voting rights in 1964 and 1965. Yet King reminded his followers that there was much ground to be covered before his dream would be fully realized. One evening in April 1968 in Tennessee, he told of how God had let him come up on the mountain:

"And I've seen the promised land. I may not get there with you. But I want you to know tonight that we, as a people, will get to the promised land." The day after he spoke these words, Martin Luther King was murdered outside his hotel room.

o Martin Luther King, Jr., Nobel Peace Prize, 1964.

Martin Luther King, Jr. at the great march in Washington, 1963.

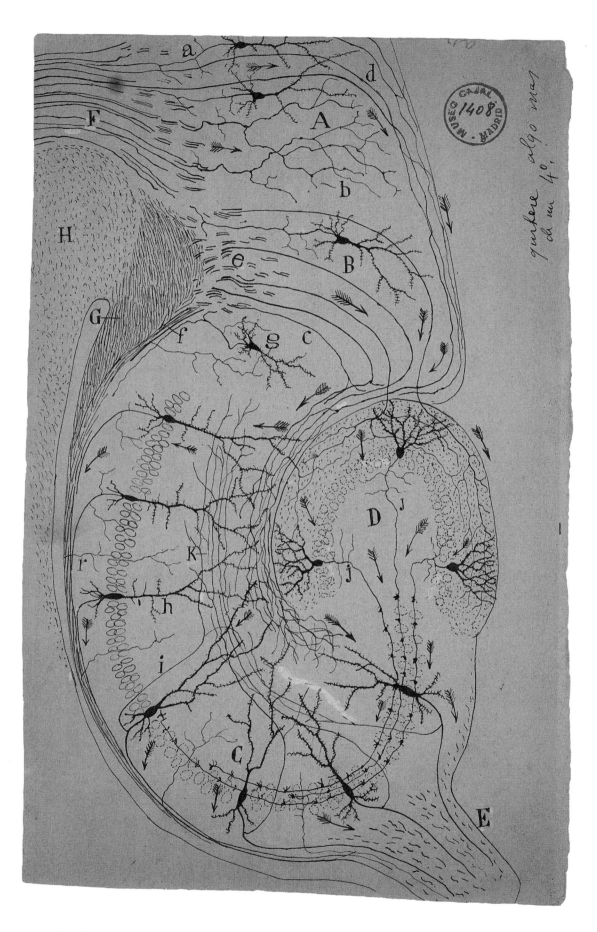

Developing an idea
Santiago Ramón y Cajal

Santiago Ramón y Cajal was the foremost pioneer of research on the nervous system. However, he had an obvious source of inspiration in Camillo Golgi. Developing and refining Golgi's technique enabled Cajal to make his great contributions to science.

During the latter half of the 1800s, scientists learned to stain various body tissues for microscopic examination. However, the methods were too haphazard to allow specific study of nerve cells. In the 1870s, Golgi had discovered that nerve cells could be specifically stained with silver nitrate. While visiting an acquaintance in Madrid in 1887, Cajal glimpsed incredible new possibilities when he was allowed to view a preparation of brain tissue that had been stained using Golgi's method. The nerve threads could be seen in absolute clarity against a transparent background. "One glance was sufficient. Stunned, I was unable to lift my gaze from the microscope."

The revelation led to a period of feverish creativity: "As new facts appeared in my preparations, ideas boiled up and jostled each other in my mind." With skill, intuition and stubbornness, Cajal adapted and improved Golgi's method. Consequently, he made discoveries that turned contemporary views on the structure and function of the nervous system upside down. A long-lasting scientific disagreement ensued between Golgi and Cajal. Eventually Cajal's ideas won general support.

Santiago Ramón y Cajal's talents were not limited to scientific research. As a child he had wanted most of all to be an artist. In fact, his sense for images and skill in sketching proved extremely useful in his scientific work. In many areas, Ramón y Cajal was self-taught. He was a pioneer in the truest sense of the word, especially in light of the technical resources of the day. His scientific production was enormous. Together with his literary works, drawings, and other pursuits, it fills nearly an entire library.

o Santiago Ramón y Cajal, Nobel Prize in Physiology or Medicine, 1906.

< Diagram illustrating the structure and connections of the hippocampus. Drawing by Santiago Ramón y Cajal, circa 1901.

Santiago Ramón y Cajal was also a devoted photographer. This is one of his self-portraits.

Leitz brass and black microscope, circa 1906, used by Santiago Ramón y Cajal.

The drawing to the right depicts the first, second, and third layers of the precentral gyrus of the cerebrum of a child of one month. Drawing by Santiago Ramón y Cajal, circa 1892.

Cajal made discoveries that turned contemporary views on the structure and function of the nervous system upside down. Most researchers of the day held that the nervous system was made up of a continuous network of cells. Cajal proposed that each cell was a separate, independent entity, ending in so-called synapses, where nerve impulses were transferred from one cell to another.

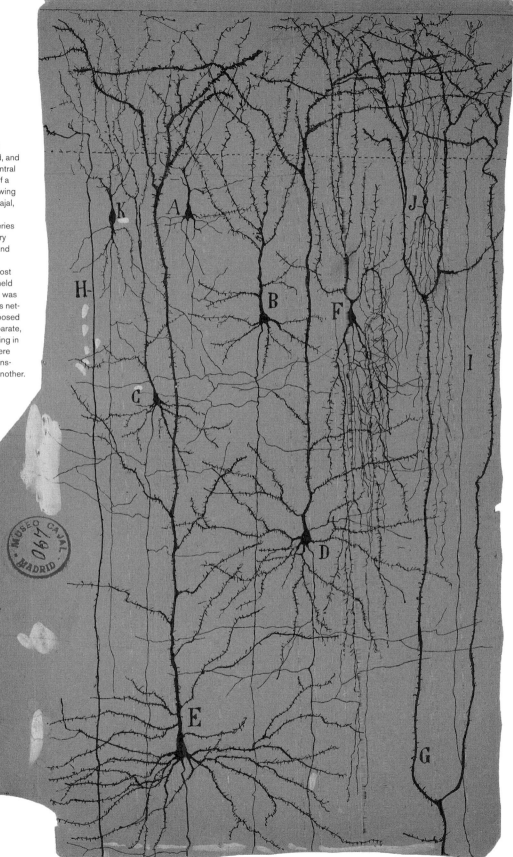

Two hats with a story. Wole Soyinka himself writes: Peripateia (from the Hunter to the Hunted)

Floppy Hat
Peripateia is the Greek expression (used especially in drama) for a reversal of fortunes. At home, my favourite form of relaxation is hunting, and I wore the faded khaki hat when I undertook my final hunt in Nigeria in November 1994, 'got lost' in the forest and surfaced in the neighbouring Republic of Benin—a fugitive from the dictatorship of Sanni Abacha. Later—on my exile circuit in African countries, Europe, the U.S. etc—the hat was pressed into service as part of a prudent disguise as I continued to evade the dictator's rather persistent agents—my head of hair being the most obvious giveaway.

Yoruba Cap
The black Yoruba cap was part of my formal attire—mostly retained in my hand—when I received the Nobel prize in 1986. It surfaced again among the wardrobe which joined me later in exile, so I added it to the other head camouflage. (I still wear a headgear on occasion, despite the end of the dictatorship, but only to enjoy some anonymity.)

While working on a project of the International Parliament of Writers, the setting up of a network of Cities of Asylum for persecuted writers, I received a complimentary ticket of a $1000 (!!!) ringside seat for a boxing match from a casino-hotelier-cum-bibliophile who was once an aspiring writer. He had spearheaded the creation of the first such city in the United States in—of all places!—Las Vegas! Again, I wore this very cap—to avoid easy recognition. After this novel and extravagant addition to its mixed fortunes, what else is left but to retire the cap, in grand style, from active service!

Wole Soyinka

Synthesis of cultures

Wole Soyinka

"God of Iron and Metallurgy, Explorer, Artisan, Hunter, God of War, Guardian of the Road, the Creative Essence." Thus reads one of Wole Soyinka's descriptions of Ogun, a god of Yoruba mythology. In other descriptions of Ogun, Soyinka uses terms from Greek mythology: Ogun corresponds to Dionysus, Apollo, and Prometheus.

Soyinka's authorship springs from the literature and mythologies of several peoples. The dynamic melding of cultures is one of the strongest aspects of his work. On the one hand, his drama is rooted in traditional African folk theater's unique combination of dance, music, and action. On the other, it is influenced by the Western heritage—the dramas of the Antique period, Shakespeare, J.M. Synge, and the modern avant garde.

One of the reasons Soyinka is able to unite different cultures with such ease is the fact that Nigeria, as he himself says, is a cultural hybrid. Home to hundreds of ethnic groups, it is one of Africa's most culturally diverse nations. Although Soyinka writes in English, he usually formulates his poems in his Yoruban mother tongue first. In transferring Yoruban language constructions into English, his literary style becomes something new.

How does Soyinka's own creative process work? He makes no claims to being a methodical writer:

"I'm not one of those writers I learned about who get up in the morning, put a piece of paper in the typewriter machine and start writing. That I've never understood. I can write days on end, not wanting to do anything else. And at other times gestate. I consider the process of gestation just as important as when you're actually sitting down putting words to the paper."

Soyinka honored at the Sorbonne, the most prestigious university in France.

Soyinka has also experienced how something in and of itself destructive can contribute to creativity. As a prisoner for several years during Nigeria's civil war, he produced some of his best work. His collection of poetry, *A Shuttle in the Crypt*, was written in the darkness of his cell on bits of paper and between the lines of books. Soyinka had to keep the creative process alive simply to maintain his sanity.

o Wole Soyinka, Nobel Prize in Literature, 1986.

Wole Soyinka in 1970.

Toni Morrison and Wole Soyinka.

Soyinka, The Lion, Storms Lagos

Continued On Page 5

Soyinka: 'Opposition Ambassador' returns today

Nigeria's only Nobel Laureate, Professor Wole Soyinka arrives home today four years after he ran into exile in 1994.

His plane will touched down at the Murtala Muhammed Airport, Ikeja at 6.30pm. He is expected to walk into an elaborate airport reception by friends, admirers and political associates.

But his schedule is hectic, as he is expected to move from the airport to Moshood Abiola Crescent, to pay his last respects to Abiola's widows and pay his last respects to Abiola's graveside.

Soyinka along with other exiles had waged a vigorous global campaign to actualise Abiola's June 12 mandate before Abiola's suspicious death 7 July brought an end to the campaign.

MAGAZINE

OCTOBER 18, 1998   PAGE M1

Kongi And The October Factor

By LOUIS ODION

"FOR me, justice is the first condition of humanity — Soyinka

It is hardly feasible to deconstruct Professor Wole Soyinka's involvement in the national epoch with its many trajectories without being stricken by the repetition of the October month.

With his triumphant homecoming Wednesday in Lagos, the supremo of words, easily regarded as the gravest security threat against the military regime in the last four years, marked a significant turn in the new search to build a common voice within vis-a-vis the higher quest for a compass to navigate the waters of national challenges ahead. A number of exiles had since arrived. A few others are yet to come. Now, the nation is being seen as one family from outside again.

Precisely twelve years ago in the month of October, Soyinka woven the spotlight for being the first African to clinch the highest honour in literature - the Nobel.

Twenty-two years earlier, again in the month of October, the *Capo of Tortuga* was at the centre of the *Mystery Gunman* saga. The story has it that a mystery gunman held up the Nigerian Broadcast Corporation, Ibadan, then the headquarters of the Western Region of Nigeria allegedly to make the studio supervisor, one Akanede Oshun, air a pre-recorded cassette dripping of anti-establishment views in place of the scheduled broadcast of the highly unpopular premier,

PHOTO: PABL

Wole Soyinka

The lion spits fire!

THE tyranny of General Sani Abacha's regime opened a new vista in the concept of democratic struggles in Nigerian exiles. Many Human Rights and Pro-Democracy ac-

had become a very big question mark for democracy movement here, which I was heading. You remember we were even planning a march on Abuja, a peaceful march to protest things like that, all

this, the press has been magnificent, really magnificent, and one of these days, when there's more pleasure we are to erect a statue, I'm going to see personally to this, that a few hundreds of the press be erected at a prominent place

Wole Soyinka's return to Nigeria after years in exile caused a furor in the Nigerian press.

Audition for the new play *King Baabu* in 2000.

Tradition and nation

William Butler Yeats

William Butler Yeats was at the center of the rapidly shifting political and cultural life of his time. He became one of the foremost figures of the new Ireland, which had freed itself from British control in the early 1900s. He found inspiration in the literature of his home country, but also in the literature of other cultures.

Yeats came from an influential and well established Protestant family of the late 1800s in Ireland. In many ways he came to symbolize the cultural renaissance underway in Irish literature in the decades at the turn of the century. He found motifs both in the struggle for freedom that shook Ireland in the middle of the first decade of the twentieth century and into the early years of the 1920s, and from ancient Celtic culture, which became an emblem in the struggle. Yeats' poetry is intimately connected with the developments leading up to Irish independence.

The blossoming of Irish nationalism brought about a serious wave of research into Irish folklore and language that spanned most of the 19th century. In the spirit of the times and thanks to the research, Yeats began to write dramas and poetry grounded in Irish legends and tales.

Over time, Yeats found his sympathies divided on the cause of nationalism. He believed in the goal—independence—but questioned the means. One of his most famous poems deals with the horror he felt upon hearing of an uprising against British authorities in 1916. The leaders of the uprising were executed. Yeats wondered, was this sacrifice necessary?

When the Irish Free State was finally formed in 1922,

‹ Portrait of William Butler Yeats by his father, John Butler Yeats.

A pair of scissors and a letter-knife of William Butler Yeats.

Yeats was elected to Parliament in appreciation for his efforts. As the leader for the new national theater in Dublin, he was important for all the new growth in Irish drama, which included names such as Synge and O'Casey. For a time, his official role in politics and cultural life were as important as his poetry.

Yeats' work was influenced by more than the traditions of his own culture. Just as nationalistic movements were prevalent around the world in that day, the occult also attracted the interest of many artists, authors, and the generally curious. Yeats, too, found himself attracted to these mysteries. He melded his fascination with Eastern cultures and religions, theosophy, and various European esoteric movements of the late 1800s into a personal belief and literary style.

o William Butler Yeats, Nobel Prize in Literature, 1923.

George de Hevesy did not always have enough time to maintain his contacts by traveling. The exchange with colleagues all over Europe demanded that chemicals be sent by mail.

Traveling as a source for inspiration

George de Hevesy

For George de Hevesy, travel was the wind beneath his wings. His travels enabled him to combine ideas he had encountered in different places. Hevesy's constant traveling, while due in part to his scientific interests, was also forced upon him by political circumstances. His family, recently elevated to nobility status, was of Jewish background. With the increased political unrest in central Europe in the early 1900s, Hevesy became one of a sizeable group of European intellectuals of Jewish descent forced to travel to escape persecution in their homelands.

The most important stops along the way during Hevesy's travels were Budapest, Freiburg, Zürich, Karlsruhe, Manchester, Vienna, Copenhagen, and Stockholm.

Perhaps Hevesy's most important discovery was that the radioactive isotopes of various basic elements could be used to study chemical processes. Hevesy conducted the major part of his research at Niels Bohr's institute in Copenhagen, although the work continued over a long period of time at a number of other locations. It all began when Ernest Rutherford in Manchester asked Hevesy to separate the isotope radium D from lead. Although Hevesy was unsuccessful at the task, it gave him the idea that since radium D could not be separated from lead, perhaps common lead could be "marked" with radium D. By observing the radiation released by the radium D, lead could be traced throughout the course of various processes. At the Radium Institute in Vienna, Friedrich Paneth had gotten a similar idea. Hevesy went to Vienna to begin a cooperative effort with him. Together they developed the method that is in use today, especially in medicine. In Copenhagen, Hevesy further developed the

method in cooperation with physiologist August Krogh.

In developing the "isotopic tracer method," Hevesy delved into a number of scientific fields—the study of radioactivity, biological processes, and the separation of isotopes. Yet circumstances outside the purely scientific were also important. The mobile lifestyle that had been forced upon him had allowed him to gather the ideas and material with which he built the foundation of his research. Hevesy's journeys took him not only to different countries, but to new places in the shifting landscapes of science.

o George de Hevesy, Nobel Prize in Chemistry, 1944.

Hafnium salts of different purities. In the 1920s some gaps remained in the periodic table of the elements. One of the gaps that scientists tried to fill was element number 72, which theoretically should exist but had not been discovered. The scientists were looking for an element resembling elements close to 72 in the periodic table, e.g. element 71, lutetium. George de Hevesy, who was working at Niels Bohr's Institute in Copenhagen at the time, instead followed Bohr's atomic model and looked for an element resembling zirconium, element 40. In collaboration with Dutch physicist Dirk Coster, he found an unknown line in the spectrum of zirconium. It turned out to come from element 72. The new element discovered was named hafnium after the old Roman name for Copenhagen.

< George de Hevesy in his laboratory in Freiburg.

"Spindle" of glass with six capillaries, used by Piotr Kapitsa around 1940 to study superfluid helium. The device is balanced on a needle in a container with liquid helium at a temperature below 2.19 Kelvin. The capillaries thus become filled with liquid. If a ray of light is focused on the device so that the liquid is heated, the spindle begins to rotate. The explanation of this phenomenon is that at temperatures below 2.19 Kelvin, liquid helium is a mixture of two liquids, a normal liquid and a quantum liquid. When heat is added, the superfluid quantum liquid is transformed into normal liquid and is squirted out through the capillaries. Because the superfluid liquid can creep in along the walls of the capillaries, this process goes on as long as heat is added.

Piotr Kapitsa and James Chadwick at Chadwick's wedding, during which Kapitsa served as "best man."

A cohesive power

Piotr Kapitsa

"I feel I am a member of a collective headed by Crocodile. I feel I am indeed turning one of the little wheels of European Science."

Piotr Kapitsa wrote these words in 1922 in a letter home to his mother in Russia. At the time, Kapitsa was at Cambridge in England, and "the Crocodile" was his nickname for his professor, Ernest Rutherford. However, Kapitsa was more than just a laborer in Rutherford's vineyard. The same year saw the beginnings of the group known as "the Kapitsa Club," which met in Kapitsa's office. "The Kapitsa Club" hosted informal lectures which led to lively discussions about the latest discoveries in physics.

During his years at the Cavendish Laboratory Kapitsa would pursue successful experimental work in several areas, first in magnetism and later on in low-temperature physics. When the new Mond Laboratory was established, the foreign-born Kapitsa became its chairman, a situation quite unusual for England at that time.

During a visit to the Soviet Union in 1934, Kapitsa was detained there. He was appointed head of a new research institute in Moscow, where he continued his work in low-temperature physics. Some of his equipment was shipped to Moscow from Cambridge, since his coworkers in England felt that they did not have much use for the apparatuses, and that Kapitsa himself was the only one who really knew how to use them properly. At his new institute, Kapitsa once again became a binding element and a source of inspiration to a new circle of colleagues.

In lectures and other venues, Kapitsa expressed his ideas on modern science. According to his view, science

Piotr Kapitsa at his desk in Cambridge.

was the result of "collective creativity" and required organization. The leading figure around whom the collective gathered was important—his role was that of a director: "he creates the spectacle, even if he does not appear on the stage." Another of Kapitsa's basic requirements was open discussion. In 1964, he expressed his concern over the climate of Soviet science: "The art, the whole culture, of discussions and scientific debates has faded in our country."

That Kapitsa was kept in the Soviet Union against his will gives an indication that his relationship with the Stalin regime was not free of conflict. He openly opposed the regime several times. Despite the repressions leveled against him, Kapitsa was nonetheless able to continue his scientific work.

o Piotr Kapitsa, Nobel Prize in Physics, 1978.

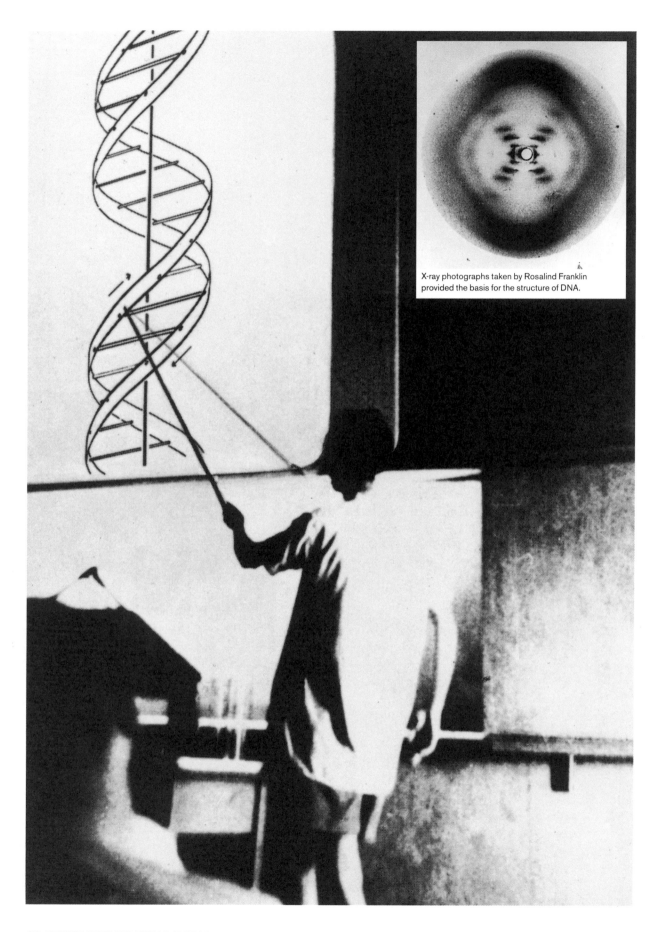

X-ray photographs taken by Rosalind Franklin provided the basis for the structure of DNA.

Conversation after conversation

Francis Crick and James D. Watson

Through conversation—or perhaps intellectual inter-play— Francis Crick and James Watson found the solution to one of the most significant scientific problems of the 1900s: the structure of the DNA molecule, and its importance for genetic inheritance.

Descriptions of how the discovery was made vary. Watson's description of life in Cambridge in his book, *The Double Helix*, gives the impression that more of their time was taken up by tea parties, pub visits, and trips than by research. More recently, however, he has also characterized his time in Cambridge as rather boring. Crick maintained that long periods of fruitless searching, interrupted by periods of intensive work are the natural rhythm of scientific research.

While Watson claimed that competition was the impetus behind their work, Crick did not agree at all. Watson's memoirs depict Linus Pauling as their greatest competitor. They worked onward in fear that Pauling would find the solution before them. According to Watson, when Pauling publicized a solution which they were convinced was faulty, their reaction was one of satisfied relief.

The key to the solution of the problem was the x-ray photographs taken by Rosalind Franklin at King's College in London. Today we may wonder why Franklin and her colleague Maurice Wilkins did not find the solution. Maurice Wilkins himself explained that "We could not cooperate."

But Crick and Watson could cooperate. When one of

< James Watson presenting the structure of the DNA molecule at Cold Spring Harbor in 1953.

James Watson and Francis Crick at their model of the DNA molecule at the Cavendish Laboratory in Cambridge.

them focused on an idea which became a dead-end, the other was able to provide new direction. The two dared to be rude and impudent to one another, and in the end, complemented one another. One characterization holds that Watson was strictly a biologist and Crick strictly a physicist. According to Crick, however, their cooperation was considerably more complex. Without fear, they delved into one another's areas of expertise, and through their untiring conversations, succeeded in uniting the knowledge which each of them held.

o Francis Crick and James D. Watson, Nobel Prize in Physiology or Medicine, 1962.

Interacting with his surroundings: Albert Einstein strolling with a friend at Princeton University in the mid-1950s. Einstein did his most revolutionary work early on in his career, however he remained important in science as well as in society in general. He figured prominently in scientific debate, among other things for his unwillingness to accept certain parts of the world view presented by quantum physics. The idea that the world was ruled by chance was foreign to him: "I cannot believe that God plays dice with the cosmos!"

Of Jewish descent, Albert Einstein was one of many scientists who fled Nazi-controlled Europe for the United States. Einstein's theories became building blocks in the development of the atomic bomb. In a famous letter to President Franklin Delano Roosevelt, he pointed out the risk that the Nazis might succeed in building an atomic bomb.

Like many other foreign scientists, Einstein remained in the USA after the end of war. The Institute for Advanced Study at Princeton, where Einstein worked is one of the Americanacademic institutions which have provided a stimulating and attractive milieu for researchers from around the world.

Books in which ideas and experiences have been collected form a background for the exchange of thoughts in Marie Louise von Motesiczky's painting *Conversation in the Library*. The painting depicts the author Elias Canetti in conversation with poet and anthropologist Franz Baermann Steiner. The painting is also an image of the mobile Central European culture. The artist Marie Louise von Motesiczky was a Viennese living in London. Steiner came from Prague, but also lived in England. Canetti was born in Bulgaria, lived in Vienna periodically, but also ended up in London. Canetti was awarded the Nobel Prize in literature "for writings marked by a broad outlook, a wealth of ideas and artistic power".

Creative Milieus

The Nobel Prizes reward individuals. Yet for most Nobel Laureates, the environments in which they have lived and worked have had great significance. The creative process is extremely dependent upon the individual's surroundings. What is it about a particular place that stimulates creativity?

Perhaps it would be better to begin with the simple question, "What is an environment?" Is the concept limited to an office, a building, a city, a country? Can it be a group of people linked together by ties other than their geographical location? An atmosphere within their social circles or an attitude in their exchange of ideas? Or the way in which life and its activities are organized?

What is characteristic of environments that foster creativity? Whether we look at cities, buildings, organizations or networks of people, similar preconditions for and hindrances to innovation seem to stand out.

One of the most important preconditions for the flourishing of creativity is knowledgeable people. Ideas and traditions require time to develop. A new development may begin in different environments, only to come to completion in a certain environment. At different points in time, certain places have shown a remarkable potential to attract persons with unique competencies.

Communication—the exchange of knowledge and ideas between individuals and areas—is important for creative results. Often, new ideas spring forth in "border areas" between different disciplines. Unexpected cross-disciplinary encounters may result in new combinations of knowledge and ideas. There is a need for informal meeting areas in cities and buildings as well as in organizations and networks. Communications and technical aids achieve their highest potential only when personal contact has been established and people have gotten to know one another.

Creative processes are encouraged by diversity and variation rather than by homogeneity and similarity. Often it seems as though radical innovation begins when a certain degree of instability and uncertainty prevail—for the individual or for society in general. Instability makes it easier to break with customary patterns of thought and systems of rules. Creativity seems to benefit more from freedom than from hierarchies and regulation.

While access to economic (and other) resources can be a prerequisite for creative activity, it is not necessarily always the decisive factor.

Can creative environments be created on purpose? Can they be planned or do they develop spontaneously?

During the course of a lifetime a person moves between environments that are meaningful to his or her development. Many have testified to the importance of their childhood and education for future work. In adult life, not only are the more limited environments of job and career important to creative work; other of life's prerequisites are of meaning as well.

The following section deals with a number of environments that have been important to Nobel Prize recipients and their work. These are not necessarily the places that claim the most Nobel Laureates. Rather, each environment presented illustrates different aspects and characteristics. Each example contributes to an understanding of what is important in the environments of science, literature and peace work.

Outdoor teaching in Santiniketan then and now.

Open sanctuary

Santiniketan

Yatra visvam bhavatyekanidam—"A place where the whole world makes a home in a single nest." This motto was coined by the great Indian poet Rabindranth Tagore, who in 1901 opened a school in Santiniketan, ca. 100 U.S. miles northwest of Calcutta. Tagore remembered his own school years with distaste: rigorous discipline, soul-numbing subjects, and obligatory studies in English. At Santiniketan, he wanted to tie into the tradition of the *ashram*—a spiritual and cultural center where students were educated outdoors in the open air. Tagore wanted to emphasize classical Indian culture while providing a modern education at the same time. Music, art, and dance were equally as important as language instruction and modern science. In addition, a school was opened for the surrounding villages, with the goal of educating and strengthening the poor farm families of the countryside.

The school in Santiniketan grew, and in 1921 saw the founding of Visva-Bharati, which would become one of India's foremost universities. In the beginning, the work was characterized by the campaign against European colonialism. Tagore and his successors wanted to create a cultural center for all of Asia. By strengthening the sense of connection between the Asian peoples, they hoped to foster improved dialogue with the West. At the same time, the school's motto reinforced thoughts on the common ties between people of all nations.

Santiniketan soon became a well-known gathering place for researchers and artists from around the world. The informal and open relationship between students and teachers made it attractive. Many stories from the first half century at Santiniketan give witness to the sense of peace and lively creativity that prevailed. Amartya Sen attended the school as a boy, as did a number of other Indian cultural personalities and politicians.

Following India's independence, Visva-Bharati came under the authority of the state in 1951. In some aspects, it became a more conventional modern university. What has happened to Tagore's dream of a very special sort of education? Does anything remain of the school's original ideals? Although answers to these questions vary, Visva-Bharati is still utterly unique in its cultural orientation. The school is one of the foremost centers in the world for Indian song and dance, and art.

The relationship between teachers and students is unusually informal, and all teachers live in residences close to the student dormitories. The younger students are still educated outside. Under tall trees that provide shade and coolness during the warm morning hours, they sit in their orange and white school uniforms, as did the first students at Santiniketan 100 years ago.

Rabindranath Tagore with a little boy.

George de Hevesy, second from left, with colleagues at the University of Budapest.

A young Eugene Wigner on Gellért hill with a view over Budapest.

George de Hevesy as a young boy.

The investigative education
Budapest

"The future will be, like the schools are today." This statement was made by Albert Szent-Györgyi, one of many well-known scientists educated in the *gymnasium* high schools of Budapest. The Gymnasium of the Piarist Order, the Fasori Lutheran Gymnasium, and the Minta Gymnasium, which became a model for other *gymnasium* schools, are among the best known.

Some of the foremost former pupils of these schools besides Szent-Györgyi are physicists Eugene Wigner, Leo Szilard, Edward Teller, and Theodore von Kármán; chemists George de Hevesy, Michael Polyani, and George Olah; mathematician John Neumann; and economist John C. Harsanyi.

What's so special about Budapest's schools? A certain elitism and a spirit of competition partly explains the successes of their students. For example, annual contests in mathematics and physics have been held since 1894. The instruction the students receive as well as these contests are an expression of a special pedagogy and a striving to encourage creativity. Mór Kármán, founder of the Minta school, believed that everything should be taught by showing its relation to everyday life. Instead of learning rules by heart from books, students tried to formulate the rules themselves.

Of course, schooling does not entirely explain the successes of the above-mentioned men of science. There are scientists from Budapest for whom school did not play an especially important role. Dennis Gabor developed his passion for physics during his youth in Budapest, but did so for the most part on his own. Georg von Békésy spent his school years in Germany and Switzer-

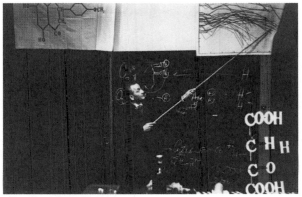
Albert Szent-Györgyi lecturing.

land, but returned to Budapest to take his doctorate.

Yet there is one aspect which all of these men have in common: each of them has made groundbreaking contributions to science while living elsewhere. Within scientific circles it has even been joked that these men of Budapest actually came from the planet Mars. They were remarkably brilliant and too unusually numerous, considering that they all came from such a small area. They spoke with an accent resembling no other, and a mother tongue no one else understood a word of.

There is a dark side to the diaspora of these Hungarian scientists. The first part of the 1900s was rife with war and political unrest. WWI was raging, the double monarchy of Austria-Hungary disintegrated, and revolution broke out. A further aspect was growing anti-Semitism. Science provided a way out. It offered "membership" in an international association, and could be practiced elsewhere in the world.

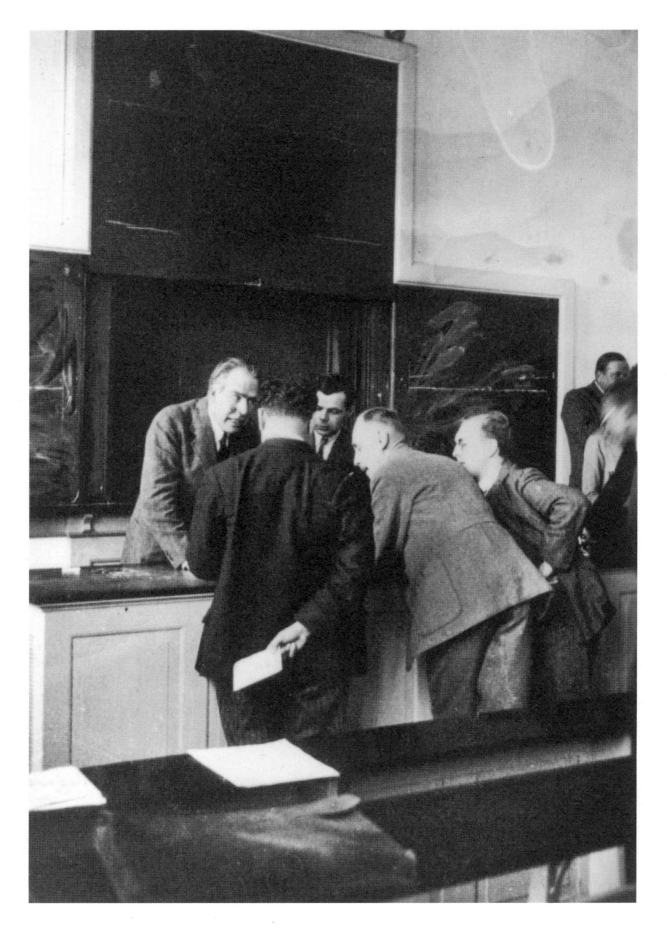

The untiring conversation

Copenhagen

Der Kopenhagener Geist—"the Copenhagen Spirit," an expression minted by Werner Heisenberg, originally referred to a certain way of tackling the problems of theoretical physics. The term later came to mean a way of working in general and the atmosphere that prevailed in the circle surrounding Niels Bohr.

Certain people seem to have the capacity to encourage ideas not only in themselves, but in others. Niels Bohr was one of those people. In the 1920s and '30s, numerous physicists, chemists, and biologists were drawn to Copenhagen in order to speak with Bohr and to experience the milieu in which he lived and worked.

Niels Bohr came from a family with a strong academic background. His father Christian Bohr was an internationally renowned scientist, and his brother Harald was an accomplished mathematician. Thanks to the atomic model that he presented in 1913, the name of Niels Bohr had become a household word in theoretical physics. His family traditions certainly helped his academic self-assurance. After having lost a competition for a professorship, he managed to establish a special chair in theoretical physics for himself at the University of Copenhagen. In 1918 he convinced the Danish parliament to finance the building of an entire institute for theoretical physics.

Many of the founders of the new physics sought out Bohr and his institute: Werner Heisenberg, Erwin Schrödinger, Paul Dirac, Wolfgang Pauli, Max Born, and many others. These scientists came from many different parts of Europe, but Copenhagen and Niels Bohr became

< Bohr engaged in intense discussion with colleagues Wolfgang Pauli, Lothar Wolfgang Nordheim, Erwin Fues and Leon Rosenfeld in 1929.

Niels Bohr and George de Hevesy at the Van de Graaf generator.

their meeting point. Bohr had a documented talent for seeing people's gifts and for finding and supporting promising young researchers. All who became involved in this process of discovery visited the brick building on Blegdamsvej Street at one point or another. All of them were infected with the feeling that they had participated

Niels Bohr, James Franck, and Hans Marius Hansen in 1921.

Niels Bohr arriving at his institute by bicycle.

Bohr's institute became a destination for physicists from all over the world, among them Japanese Yoshio Nishina and Indian Bidhi Busan Ray.

Hans Marius Hansen, Niels Bohr, and Paul Ehrenfest in the institute library.

in something great, and that they had had a hand in creating something new.

Bohr was far from a brilliant lecturer. Instead, he constantly needed to converse with other physicists. In these conversations, he tried to determine partly his own thoughts and partly the thoughts that his conversation partners had. Stories are told of how he could wander around hour after hour with his pipe, mumbling as he tried to clarify and purify the basic characteristics of a problem. The more important were the things he had to say, the more he mumbled and fiddled with his pipe.

Niels Bohr and Albert Einstein could immerse themselves completely in conversation and forget time and space in their most practical, concrete sense. One anecdote tells that during a visit Einstein made to Copenhagen, they took a streetcar to Bohr's institute. However, they became so involved in conversation that they forgot to get off when they reached their stop. Several stops later, they got off and took the streetcar back, but became lost in conversation again, and rode too far in the other direction. The procedure was repeated several times before they finally remembered to get off at the correct stop.

These conversations were not limited to the Institute, but continued at Bohr's summer home in Tisvilde, north of Copenhagen, on long walks or on boat trips. The atmosphere was an intimate one in which Bohr's entire family participated.

The atmosphere at the institute was unusually informal for the time. Otto Robert Frisch related that when he arrived for a seminar, he was greeted by the sight of Lev Landau lying on his back on a table, deep in discussion. Bohr did not seem to see anything odd about this. It took time to become accustomed to the habits of the institute, where nothing else mattered except the ability to think clearly.

Discussions with Bohr could also be taxing. Heisenberg told of one episode in which Erwin Schrödinger's health was put at risk. In 1926 while in Munich, Heisenberg and Schrödinger happened into a conversation on the interpretation of wave mechanics, which revealed that their opinions were diametrically opposed. Heisenberg later wrote to Bohr, who invited both him and Schrödinger to Copenhagen. The discussions between Bohr and Schrödinger began at the train station and continued

Bohr at the blackboard.

For several years physicists traveled to Copenhagen to attend conferences arranged by Niels Bohr. Above, Wolfgang Pauli, Werner Heisenberg, and Niels Bohr can be seen at the center of a picture from a conference in 1936. Below, the three are involved in a discussion at the same conference.

uninterrupted. The usually amiable Bohr could at times become fanatical and unconciliatory—which happened at that time. He was not prepared to accommodate his opponent in the least, and refused to tolerate the minutest lack of clarity. The discussions continued day and night without either party reaching agreement on any point. Schrödinger was staying with Bohr and his family, and thus found little respite. He became sick from overexertion and took to his bed with a fever. Mrs. Margrethe Bohr nursed him and served him tea and cookies. Niels Bohr, however, sat on the edge of Schrödinger's bed, verbally attacking him: "But surely you must realize that..."

Heisenberg himself lived for several years in the Institute's attic apartment, with a view over Copenhagen's Fælled Park. The Bohr family's villa was located in the same neighborhood. Bohr would often visit Heisenberg for nighttime discussions that would last until both of them were weary. Yet these discussions also helped Bohr develop his theory of complementarity, and Heisenberg to develop his theory of uncertainty.

Despite the strains, Niels Bohr created an intellectual oasis for his many visitors, which even became a sanctu-ary during times of world strife. After WWI, Copenhagen was untouched by the battles and political uneasiness that plagued much of the rest of Europe, especially Germany, where quantum mechanics had its birthplace in Munich and Göttingen. Later in the 1930s, many of Bohr's friends fled the Nazis and the war and found refuge in Copenhagen. Some stayed, but most of them traveled on to England or the United States with Bohr's help. In 1943, Bohr himself was forced to flee, and did not return until after the end of the war.

In establishing new research institutes, many have sought to recapture the creative atmosphere that surrounded Niels Bohr. Max Delbrück, who had spent time in Copenhagen during the 1930s, was one of them. He tried to create something similar at the California Institute of Technology and even during his summers at Cold Spring Harbor. There, James Watson was also influenced. Delbrück also passed on the ideal to Niels Jerne and Fritz Melchers, who tried to encourage this attitude toward research at the Basel Institute for Immunology.

Encounters in the harbor of nature

Cold Spring Harbor

"As the summer passed on I liked Cold Spring Harbor more and more, both for its intrinsic beauty and for the honest ways in which good and bad science got sorted out." Thus James D. Watson, one of the discoverers of the DNA spiral, described his first experiences of Cold Spring Harbor.

Cold Spring Harbor is located on Long Island in New York, a little over a half an hour from Pennsylvania Station on Manhattan. Descriptions of the natural beauty of this place are numerous. It offers greenery, a natural harbor, and opportunities for sailing and swimming in the waters of the Atlantic.

In the field of biology Cold Spring Harbor is famous for its research laboratory, which has attracted a number of the most prominent scientists of the 20th century. Some of the most well known researchers at the laboratory have included Barbara McClintock, who discovered "jumping genes," and Alfred D. Hershey, another of the pioneers of genetics. Although James D. Watson, mentioned above, had already made his groundbreaking discoveries regarding the structure of DNA by the time he came to Cold Spring Harbor, he served as head of the laboratory for a long period.

Cold Spring Harbor is important not only for its own research; it has also served as an appealing meeting place. In the pioneer days of molecular biology in the 1940s and 50s, biologists from around the world spent the summer months at Cold Spring Harbor, socializing and discussing ideas. Here one could meet people of like mind, start new friendships and begin cooperative research

< Alfred D. Hershey and James D. Watson sailing.

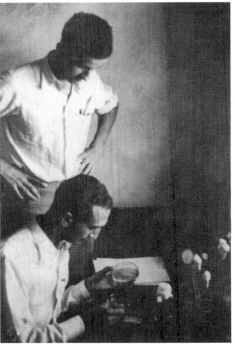

Max Delbrück and Salvador Luria in 1941.

efforts which could then continue throughout the year. In fact, one of the scientists most often associated with Cold Spring Harbor, Max Delbrück, was not a permanent fixture there, but a summer guest.

Max Delbrück has been called "the founder of molecular biology." He has also jokingly been referred to as Niels Bohr's greatest contribution to biology. As a young physicist in Berlin in the 1930s, he came into contact with Niels Bohr and was influenced by Bohr's attempts to ana-

Picnic at Jones Beach on the south coast of Long Island in 1941. W. Stanley, Max Delbrück, A.E. Mirskey, and J.W. Gowen.

Max Delbrück at the chessboard with his wife Manny.

Max Delbrück and André Lwoff in 1946.

D. Shemin, A.H. Doermann, Dorothy Crowfoot Hodgkin, and J.F. Taylor in 1948.

lyze the processes of life using the methods of physics and mathematics. Judging by the number of Nobel laureates and the fantastic developments in molecular biology in the years following WWII, Delbrück succeeded in duplicating Bohr's magic. An entirely new branch of science and a whole new view of our world grew forth in an inspiring, creative and tolerant environment.

At his home department at the California Institute of Technology in Pasadena, Delbrück and his colleagues tried to re-create the atmosphere of Bohr's Copenhagen. Bohr's attitude toward science also inspired the special, intensive atmosphere of intellectual exchange at the laboratory at Cold Spring Harbor.

For many, summer at Cold Spring Harbor was the high point of the year. Leisure and work flowed together there. People labored together, played baseball, swam, canoed, sailed, gathered crabs and clams, ate and drank at the bar in town, or just rested on the lawn. The mysteries of the new biology permeated each activity.

The laboratory's work on bacteriophages proved of great importance to later progress in molecular biology. Bacteriophages are one of the types of organisms best suited to the study of genetic inheritance. Max Delbrück, Salvador Luria and Alfred D. Hershey made up the core of a group formed to pursue this research, "the bacteriophage group." Hershey was permanently active at Cold

Alfred Hershey in his laboratory.

James D. Watson in 1953.

Barbara McClintock and Jacques Monod.

Spring Harbor, while Delbrück and Luria were regular guests. Delbrück later described their work together:

"I mean, it was a group only in the sense that we all communicated with each other. And that the spirit was— open. This was copied straight from Copenhagen, and the circle around Bohr so far as I was concerned. In that the first principle had to be openness. That you tell each other what you are doing and thinking, and that you don't care who—who has the priority."

Without a doubt, Delbrück was the group's central figure, due not so much to his ability to choose good colleagues, but rather more to the fact that such people sought him out. Salvador Luria said that "To spend the days chewing on a problem, and writing and erasing things on the blackboard with him, is terribly exciting."

With the rapid developments in biology, the nature of work in this field has changed. The openness and creative spirit of the pioneer days is less prevalent. Economic interests, patent disputes, and competition have become more common ingredients of work in biology today. Yet there is still much more to discover. Molecular biology has entered a new phase, and Cold Spring Harbor remains an important and inspiring place for those studying the mysteries of life.

Roger Guillemin   *Niki de Saint Phalle*

In 1993 the director of the Basel Institute for Immunology, Fritz Melchers, asked the artist Niki de Saint Phalle to design the cover of the annual report, saying it should have something to do with the immune system. Niki de Saint Phalle turned to Roger Guillemin, Nobel Laureate in medicine but also a computer artist, who helped to put "a beautiful Immunological Robe" on the sculpture *Gwendolyn*. "We had great fun. The marriage of art and science."

Freedom and resources

Basel Institute for Immunology

"A paradise for a scientist!" is a phrase often used to describe the Basel Institute for Immunology. During the 1970s, visiting the newly established institute became something of a pilgrimage for biomedical researchers. Academic freedom, tremendous resources, a lack of ingrown bureaucracy, and stimulating cooperation made it highly attractive.

Basel is a city with ancient traditions of learning. The university here, Switzerland's oldest, was founded in 1460. Even so, the Institute for Immunology became something of an island in this ancient city of culture. Most of the researchers there were recruited from other parts of the world. They developed strong bonds amongst themselves, and often worked late into the night. Among the Institute's foremost members were Nobel Prize winners-to-be Niels Jerne, Georges Köhler, and Susumu Tonegawa.

Paul and Maja Sacher played a significant role in establishing the Institute. Maja Sacher, a sculptress, was widowed early on in her marriage to one of the founders of the pharmaceutical firm Hoffman-La Roche. Paul Sacher was a prominent orchestral director who also happened to have a knack for business. Upon his marriage to Maja, he became involved in Roche, serving for many years on its board of directors. The company's great successes in pharmaceuticals allowed it to support science and the arts beyond the strict areas of its business. Paul and Maja Sacher played a significant role in these efforts. At the Institute for Immunology, they were counted as friends.

The Sachers saw to it that the environs of the Institute did not lack quality artwork. The grounds are home to

Niki de Saint Phalle and Paul Sacher in front of the sculpture *Gwendolyn*, a symbol of a creative mythological goddess.

Jean Tinguely's elegant spiral *Double Helix* and Niki De Saint Phalle's voluptuous sculpture *Gwendolyn*. At the dedication ceremony for *Gwendolyn*, Paul Sacher said that the meeting between these works of art would remind all who come to the Institute that true creativity is the marriage between art and science—a view not at all foreign to the researchers at the Institute. Immunologists find it

Niels Jerne became the first director of the Basel Institute for Immunology. When Jerne took the position, he stopped his experimental work completely and concentrated on theoretical work and evaluation and reviewing of research by other scientists. Jerne had an impressive general view and devoted a lot of time to conversations on different subjects. But he did not often show up in the laboratories. One of his collaborators once wanted him to come and discuss the spaces for animals at the site. Jerne preferred to discuss the problems over "a map, plan, blueprint of the space." "I don't want to go down, the reality would confuse me."

easy to wax eloquent about the beauty of the body's sophisticated systems of defense and adaptation against foreign substances. The quest to understand the inner workings of the body yields more than fascinating insights—it is also an esthetic experience.

Throughout its thirty-year existence, from 1970 to 2000, the Institute has been financed entirely by Roche. However, the Institute is not tied to the company's research and development efforts, and has had full academic freedom. The research projects are chosen by the researchers themselves.

The Institute also had an unusual inner organization. Initially Roche had planned a conventional structure, with departments, sections, and units, but Niels K. Jerne, who was appointed the Institute's first director, had another idea. All of the researchers (referred to as "members") were equal. Divisions of authority into departments and hierarchical levels were avoided altogether. A few doubted that this horizontal organization could be maintained, and claimed that sooner or later a pyramid-shaped organization would make itself evident. However, even under the leadership of Jerne's successor, Fritz Melchers, the horizontal structure was kept for as long as the Institute existed.

The chairman would decide who would be invited to the Institute, but would have no say in deciding the individual scientist's choice of research. Each researcher received the assistance of a laboratory technician and access to other common resources. The laboratory technicians were given more responsibility than usual. Everyone was to participate in the intellectual life of the Institute. This model may be seen as an attempt to create a sort of scientific democracy; however, in principle, Niels Jerne had an elitist view of science. He believed that

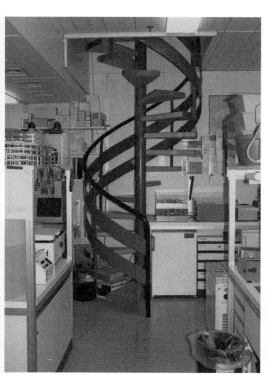

Jean Tinguely's sculpture *Double Helix* embellishes the yard of the Basel Institute for Immunology.

The social life of the institute was extensive. Many parties provided members an opportunity to exhibit their varied talents.

To enhance communication between the scientists, Jerne decided that spiral staircases should be built between the floors.

one brilliant researcher was more important than many mediocre ones. Nonetheless, he was convinced that communication and intellectual exchange were driving forces behind scientific progress.

When plans were being drawn up for the building, Jerne was afraid that members on the different floors of the two-story building would not speak to one another. Because of this he insisted that there be spiral staircases between the laboratories on the two floors. By overstaffing the institute and seeking a feeling of "crowdedness," he hoped to increase communication.

Jerne himself loved to talk. Chance meetings between individuals were a theme not only in Jerne's understanding of life and his view of how science developed. It was also a theme in his scientific theories and in his view of how the immune system functions. Jerne related that the Institute's organizational structure was based on biological systems, more specifically on the immune system itself. It is an entity made up of various parts, which achieves a dynamic equality through exchange, transformation, and arrivals and departures.

The idea of constant, ongoing conversation and unstilted, light-hearted exchange of thoughts reminds us of the ideals of Niels Bohr. In Copenhagen, Niels Jerne had come into contact with Bohr, as well as Max Delbrück, who in turn had been inspired by Bohr. Jerne's successor, Fritz Melchers, one of the Institute's first researchers, had also been inspired by Max Delbrück, who had been his teacher in Cologne. In the years that have followed, this scientific ideal of engaging conversation and a non-judgmental attitude has been transplanted again and again across the fields of science.

François Jacob, Jacques Monod, and André Lwoff after the Nobel Prize announcement in 1965.

François Jacob and the staff gathered together.

Imagination and questioning

The Pasteur Institute

"The Pasteur Institute was the Mecca of biology; the seat of innumerable discoveries; the laboratory of eminent researchers." François Jacob relates in his autobiography how he bubbled with pride and happiness when in 1949, at the beginning of his career as a research scientist, he was informed that he had received a scholarship at the renowned Pasteur Institute in Paris.

The Pasteur Institute is named after its founder Louis Pasteur, one of the great scientists of the 19th century. Pasteur pioneered the field of microbiology in the 1880s, when he succeeded in finding a vaccine against rabies. Rabies was one of the worst diseases of the day, and an international fundraising effort made it possible for Pasteur to treat patients afflicted with rabies.

Eventually the Pasteur Institute developed into a research institution covering a number of broader areas within biology. Pasteur was able to gather a circle of colleagues with the same enthusiasm and energy he himself had, and succeeded in building up an environment where research could flourish and thrive.

The typical Pasteur researcher has found himself on the periphery of more official career paths, writes François Jacob. "He was a doctor without a practice, a pharmacist without a dispensary, a chemist without an industry, an academic without a chair." From the beginning, researchers from a variety of disciplines have been brought together at the Institute. The Institute's position as a private foundation has given it flexibility and the capacity to deal with the unexpected, which public institutions sometimes lack.

Even after its establishment, private donations have

François Jacob at his microscope.

been an important resource, although today the Pasteur Institute also receives government support. Some resources come from industry, which in return may benefit from the Institute's research. The combination of in-depth science and medically adaptable activity was an idea that Pasteur himself promoted from the outset. Much research has been tied to specific diseases; for example, Nobel Prize recipients-to-be Alphonse Laveran and Charles Nicolle studied malaria and typhus, respectively.

The Pasteur Institute has an international flavor.

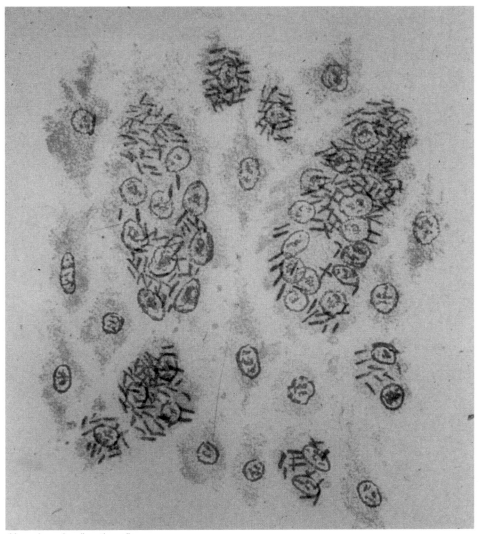

Macrophages invading other cells.

Many of the Institute's researchers have come from other countries, including Ilya Mechnikov from Russia, Jules Bordet from Belgium, and Daniel Bovet from Switzerland. Pasteur Institutes were also established in other countries, for example in Tunisia where Charles Nicolle was active, and in Belgium, where Jules Bordet returned to lead a new institute.

Since its founding, the Pasteur Institute has fostered cutting-edge research. The years following WWII were a golden age, with work being done by researchers such as André Lwoff, Jacques Monod, and François Jacob. In his description of his first seminar at the Institute, François Jacob paints a lively picture of the Pasteur Institute in those days. The guest speaker was the American Sol Spiegelman, whose ideas were meeting with resistance. The atmosphere reminded Jacob of a bullfight. Jacques Monod was the one holding the sword:

"The deathblow came later in a café on the Boulevard Pasteur, among glasses of beer. Toward the end of his talk, Spiegelman had presented a theory of which I understood nothing. What I did understand, however, was that in the café the theory was dissected, torn apart, shredded into pieces. Bit by bit, the bull weakened. A final thrust of Monod's *descabello*. The bull's final spasm. And resistance ceased. All this amid laughter and joking."

Jacob left his first seminar at the Pasteur Institute both shocked and fascinated:

"It was a surprise, that first seminar. I left both dazed and fascinated. This universe of research, still charged with mystery, suddenly appeared in a new light. This was not the cold, studious, stiff, slightly sad, slightly boring world one often imagines. But, on the contrary, a world full of gaiety, of the unexpected, of curiosity, of imagination. A life animated as much by passion as by logic. With its coteries and its own community, its idols and its taboos, its codes and rites. With its struggles, too. The

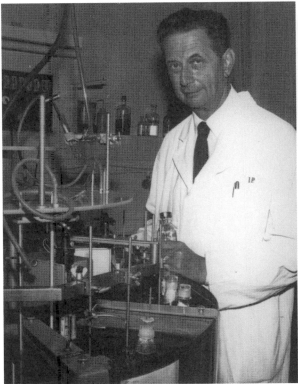

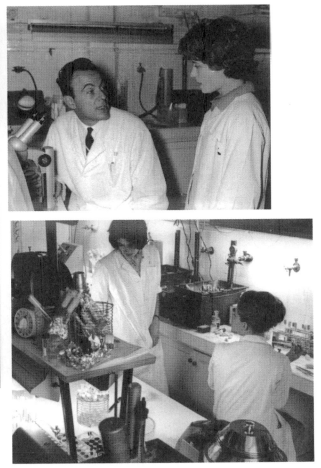

André Lwoff and François Jacob had their laboratories in the attic of the Pasteur Institute.

competition for primacy: not for temporal power but for intellectual power, dominance over the group."

Jacob worked in André Lwoff's laboratories in the attic of the Institute. The research dealt with bacteriophages, a type of primitive organism well suited to studies in genetics. Here ideas abounded and were immediately vented:

"Hardly had the results been checked than one had to draw conclusions from them, to prepare what would come next. Which, most often, took place in the public square: that is, in the corridor. The corridor was in effect the obligatory passage, the general meeting place, the agora. Everyone came there to get some item from a cupboard, or to pass round some new journal article; to relate successes or failures, to ask about the others' results; to seek advice or a chemical formula, to talk over some theory, or simply to chat. The minute they were obtained, the results of an experiment were immediately transmit-

ted to the people in the corridor. There, they were dissected, cut up, chopped fine by one person or another."

The creative milieu at the Pasteur Institute was a world where everything was constantly questioned, but at the same time very stimulating. François Jacob was not frightened away: "But for my fear of being incapable of playing a role in science, I found myself at ease in this world of dream and of doubt." Yet Jacob would play a role in science. Together with Lwoff, Monod, and others, he became one of the innovators of modern biology, one of those who through the study of microorganisms have begun mapping the structure and functions of the molecules that make up all living organisms.

The Pasteur Institute continues to expand the horizons of microbiology.

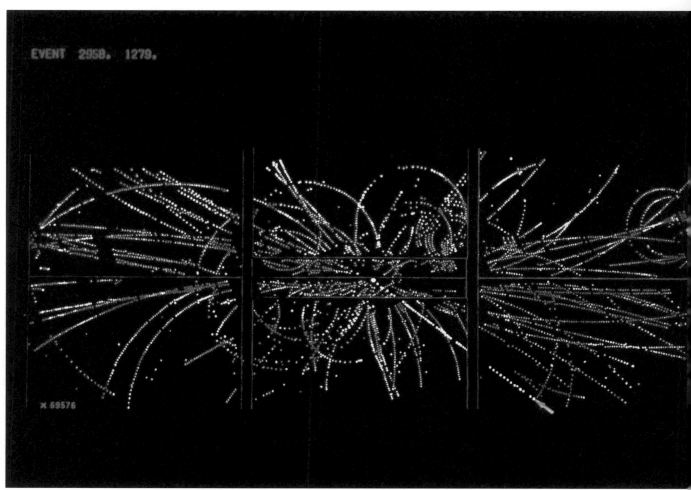

Tracks of particles created by the collision of a proton and an antiproton. Through these charts the existence of the W and Z particles could be confirmed.

Prototype detector for the UA1 experiment.

Men and machines

CERN

Just outside Geneva lies the European Organization for Nuclear Research, better known by the acronym CERN. In CERN's laboratories, offices, and auditoriums, hundreds of researchers from countries around the world are at work. Thoughts and ideas are exchanged in cafeterias, break rooms, and corridors. The languages of many nations can be heard, although English, spoken with different accents, dominates. Another common language at CERN is the language of science. It is a language without a homeland, consisting mainly of symbols and pictures. In the lunchroom, a tray riding the dirty dish conveyor exhibits a napkin full of scribbled experiment sketches and formulas.

CERN gives a certain impression that it is a place full of people, and to a certain extent it is. They are needed to undertake the enormous projects that are necessary in experimental particle physics today. Yet the underground areas are more sparsely populated. Atomic nuclei are held together by incredibly strong forces, and breaking them requires gigantic apparatuses. Researchers and technicians ride bicycles or even small trains to travel between the various parts of their machines. The largest machine, where electrons and positrons are accelerated and then allowed to collide, forms a ring measuring 27 kilometers in diameter, and stretches a bit beyond the French border.

Such large-scale research requires enormous resources, beyond the reach of most countries. One of the ideas behind CERN is the distribution of costs between several nations.

A number of prominent physicists have worked here. Among some of the best known are Georges Charpak, Carlo Rubbia, and Simon van der Meer.

Particle physics is continuously discussed in the outdoor cafeteria of CERN.

One of the most important breakthroughs in the history of CERN was the discovery of W and Z particles. These so-called massive vector bosons mediate weak interactions, one of the most basic forces of nature. Among other things, weak interactions cause beta decay, in which a neutron in an atomic nucleus is transformed into a proton and an electron.

Carlo Rubbia introduced the idea that these particles could be observed by using a particle accelerator to store protons and antiprotons. This would allow protons and antiprotons to collide. During the violent collision the sought-after particles would be freed. An important prerequisite for carrying out this experiment was Simon van der Meer's invention of stocastic cooling, a method for "packing" and storing particles.

When he presented his idea in 1976, Rubbia was working in the United States, but he moved to CERN at the

The so-called antiproton horn was invented by Simon van der Meer to focus particle beams.

Carlo Rubbia and Simon van der Meer celebrate the Nobel Prize announcement in 1984.

The UA1 experiment, which verified the existence of the W and Z particles, demanded the use of huge equipment.

critical point in time. The situation there was difficult, since several member nations wanted to reduce their economic contributions. CERN had not achieved as many scientific breakthroughs as had been hoped. It was decided to concentrate on Rubbia's project, which came to be known as the pp̄ experiment, since it did not require exorbitant resources and held scientific promise. Another factor was competition with Fermilab in the United States, which had begun its own experiment to find W and Z particles at the same time as CERN. The competition continued until the spring of 1978, when newly appointed Fermilab head Leon Lederman decided to abandon the race.

UA1, as the larger of the two sub-experiments in Project pp̄ were called, led to the confirmation of the exis-

tence of W and Z particles. The experiment was a huge success for CERN and Carlo Rubbia.

Rubbia stood out in his role as a provider of ideas and inspiration, but he was also an organizer—something of a creative steamroller. Simon van der Meer was also important to the success of the experiment. And of course the entire experiment was built upon the work of the other physicists and engineers who together succeeded in mastering such a gigantic project.

The UA1 experiment provides a telling picture of research in the late 1900s: on the one hand, huge scale, international organization, and high technology, and on the other, strong, unique individuals. This is also characteristic of the environment at CERN.

Wire chamber detector. The invention of the wire chamber and other detectors resulted in Georges Charpak being awarded the Nobel Prize in physics of 1992.

J.C. Sens, G. Charpak, T. Müller, F.J.M. Farley, and A. Zicchichi at the blackboard in 1961.

Eleven representatives of different branches of the Chicago School of Economics, who have been awarded The Bank of Sweden Prize in Economic Sciences in Memory of Alfred Nobel: Tjalling C. Koopmans, Milton Friedman, Theodore W. Schultz, George J. Stigler, James M. Buchanan, Jr., Harry M. Markowitz, Merton H. Miller, Ronald H. Coase, Gary S. Becker, Robert W. Fogel, Robert E. Lucas, Jr.

School of thought as environment?

The Chicago School of Economics

"It is a good rule that a scientist has only one chance to become successful in influencing his science, and that is when he influences his contemporaries. If he is not heeded by his contemporaries, he has lost his chance: brilliant work that is exhumed by a later generation may make the neglected scientist famous, but it will not have made him important."

Thus wrote economist George J. Stigler. For Stigler, a fundamental component of scientific activity was the exchange of ideas between colleagues. As a leading representative for the school of thought in economics known as "the Chicago School," he became an economist of great influence.

Stigler was active at the University of Chicago, an American university that can claim a significant number of Nobel laureates. In regard to the Prize in Economics in Memory of Alfred Nobel, Chicago clearly dominates. Nearly half the Nobel laureates in economics have had ties to this university at some point during their career. Many of the recipients of the Prize in Economics who had no permanent ties to the University of Chicago have in some way or another been a part of the environment there. Even economists from other institutions have been counted as part of the Chicago School.

"The Chicago School" is a rather loosely used concept. While the group has undergone several phases in its characteristics since its beginnings in the 1920s, it has always remained unique and influential. Throughout these various periods, the Chicago School has also received considerable criticism. It faced some of its sharpest opposition during the phase of the school formulated by George

George J. Stigler.

Stigler, among others. Critics have argued that economic liberalism has been used to support imperialism and the impoverishment of the Third World.

In any case, it is clear that the Department of Economics at the University of Chicago not only originated an important school of thought, it has also been a stimulating environment. Milton Friedman, another leading Chicago economist, writes that his arrival in Chicago at the beginning of the 1930s opened new realms to him. Researchers from all over the world had created "a cosmopolitan and vibrant intellectual atmosphere of a kind that I had never dreamed existed. I have never recovered."

In economic science, the University of Chicago has played and still plays several roles: it is a place of work, a meeting place for ideas, and a school of thought.

Lawrence and the staff at the magnet of the 60-inch cyclotron in 1938.

Ernest O. Lawrence.

Lawrence encourages laboratory workers during WW II.

On the road to big science

Berkeley

There was a time when people were drawn to California by the lure of gold—and by the dream of a different and more exciting life. California has retained its powers of attraction. What it is that attracts people has changed in many ways, but certain characteristics remain. Freedom from convention, the joy of life, and a comfortable climate still appeal to people from throughout the world.

The difference between east and west in the United States is greater than many people believe, even in the field of academics. For chemist Ahmed Zewail, originally from distant Egypt, the move from Philadelphia in the east to Berkeley in the west was a major upheaval: "Culturally, moving from Philadelphia to Berkeley was almost as much of a shock as the transition from Alexandria to Philadelphia—Berkeley was a new world!" Doctoral students there had mannerisms and a way of speaking that Zewail had not seen before. "Berkeley was a great place for science—the BIG science."

Many of the great names in 20th century science have worked at California's universities, of which Berkeley, across the Bay from San Francisco, is one of the most notable. Over the years there have been 17 Nobel Prize recipients with ties to Berkeley. The university's Nobel Laureates each receive a private parking space on campus. The university is broad in scope. Poet, novelist and Nobel Laureate Czeslaw Milosz is one of the prominent humanists who have had ties to Berkeley. Yet most of the university's Nobel Prize recipients specialize in physics and the branches of physics bordering on chemistry, biology, and medicine.

Berkeley's great successes in science began with physi-

View of the Lawrence Berkeley Laboratory and University of California, Berkeley.

cist Ernest O. Lawrence, who in 1928 came to Berkeley from Yale, one of the elite universities on the U.S. East Coast. In a shack at Berkeley, Lawrence built the first version of his invention, the cyclotron. In this machine, electrically charged particles could be accelerated to extreme velocities. The particles could be used to bombard atomic nuclei in order to break them down and create new isotopes and materials. This paved the way for a wealth of new discoveries in atomic physics.

But Lawrence was not only, and perhaps not even primarily, an inventor. He was also a brilliant entrepreneur and an enthusiastic leader. The research he sought to pursue was large scale and required great resources. From private donors, foundations, and the university he succeeded in gathering funds on a scale that had never been seen before in scientific research. Lawrence's success was all the more remarkable because the laboratory was built during the most severe years of the Great Depression.

Scientists posing with newly completed 60-inch cyclotron: Donald Cooksey, Ernest O. Lawrence, R. Thornton, J. Backus, W. Salisbury, and, on top of the cyclotron, Luis Alvarez and Edwin McMillan.

Lawrence surrounded himself with a group of promising researchers. At the end of 1930s Glenn T. Seaborg joined the laboratory. Seaborg and McMillan would work together on the discovery of a number of basic elements. The first two, which were called neptunium and plutonium, would be followed by eight more, including berkelium, named after Berkeley, and lawrencium, named in honor of Lawrence.

This research also forged new unions between different disciplines—physics, chemistry, biology, and medicine were united in one field of research. The possibility of using radioactive isotopes to study the route of various materials through biological processes meant that they could be used in medical research. With the help of the cyclotron, radioactive isotopes with specially adapted characteristics could be created. Another example of biochemical research at Lawrence's laboratory is Melvin Calvin's studies of plant photosynthesis with the help of the radioactive carbon isotope C-14.

During WWII, most of the scientists associated with Lawrence worked within various segments of the American atomic bomb project. The war brought a great influx of European scientists to the United States. Just before the outbreak of the war, Italian physicist Emilio Segrè came to Berkeley. He would eventually stay. Together with others, including Owen Chamberlain, Segré contributed to the discovery of the antiproton.

With WWII, a more formal and hierarchical organization also came to the laboratory. Despite the comparatively large-scale research, much of the work during the 1930s had been pursued on the basis of informal cooperation. The first organizational chart of the laboratory was drawn up in 1942, and the organization continued to grow. Today the Lawrence Berkeley National Laboratory is a large research institution. While its environment may not be as unique as it was during its pioneer days, the laboratory remains a haven for creative research.

Luis Alvarez, circa 1938, just before the identification of helium-3.

Lawrence slumps from fatigue during WW II.

Stan Thompson and Glenn Seaborg shortly before their discovery of californium in 1948.

The rowing matches are among the recurrent events in Cambridge. At the top, an oar that symbolizes the success of Cambridge University in science. Below oarsmen on the river Cam.

Community and competition
Cambridge

Cambridge is a beautiful city whose image has been inseparable from its university since the Middle Ages. Here the shifting ideals of the centuries have merged into a harmonic unity. The university's oldest buildings resemble medieval castles, with their gray granite walls and small, irregular windows. Later, beautiful brick buildings were built, with decorative wooden windows, and eventually, light, straight impressive stone palaces. During the 1900s, glass and steel replaced stone and brick. In the buildings of Cambridge, past and present meet.

Old and new meet even in the organization of academic life. Like most such educational institutions, the university is divided into various faculties, departments, and laboratories. Yet much of life in Cambridge circulates around its ancient colleges. Here teachers and students meet, and here they take their meals, both grand feasts as well as everyday lunches.

Several colleges have green meadows running down to the River Cam. In summer cows graze in the pastures, and in the city's parks bicyclists mix with football players and walkers. In springtime, one can stroll along the river and see rowers gliding along in light wooden shells. A feeling of peace prevails.

Yet appearances can be deceiving. The rowers are actually in hard training; each year they compete against Oxford, a contest undertaken in deep earnest. Members of a losing rowing team may be exposed to biting criticism.

Conditions are equally as rigorous for the researchers who work at Cambridge. The foremost talents are attracted to this place, the brightest academic stars—not

The old Cavendish Laboratory.

just from England, but from the entire world. Someone has said that Cambridge is like an island, but an island everyone wants to swim to, rather than escape from.

A small island does not have room for everyone. Those wishing to obtain a position at Cambridge must work hard and constantly show new results. Only the best can remain here. More than 70 Nobel Prize recipients acknowledge some sort of tie to Cambridge.

Ernest Walton with an unknown woman on the river Cam.

Ernest Rutherford, Mary Rutherford, Ralph Howard Fowler, and Niels Bohr at the river Cam.

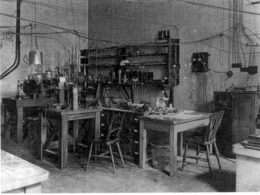

Patrick M.S. Blackett, Piotr Kapitsa, Paul Langevin, Ernest Rutherford, and C.T.R. Wilson outside the Cavendish Laboratory in 1929.

Ernest Rutherford's laboratory.

The university's activities cover many areas, but physics and the related disciplines of chemistry and biology seem to have an especially strong foothold in Cambridge. A number of the most prominent scientists of the 20th century have worked at the Cavendish Laboratory. Among the leading figures at the Laboratory have been J.J. Thomson, who discovered the electron; Ernest Rutherford, who laid the foundations of the atomic model; and Lawrence Bragg, one of the pioneers of x-ray crystallography.

At the Cavendish, Russian Piotr Kapitsa formed his Kapitsa Club, where the latest discoveries in physics were discussed. Here C.T.R. Wilson developed his cloud chamber, which led to new discoveries of the innermost makeup of matter. Francis William Aston showed the occurrence of various isotopes of basic elements. James Chadwick discovered the neutron and John Cockcroft and Ernest Walton split the lithium atom. Martin Ryle and Anthony Hewish made groundbreaking discoveries in radio astrophysics.

Under the leadership of Lawrence Bragg from the late

1930s onward, research at the Cavendish worked its way toward the bordering disciplines of chemistry and biology. Bragg, together with his father William Henry Bragg, had developed x-ray crystallography into a powerful tool for determining chemical structures. Others who joined the laboratory at this time included Max Perutz, John Kendrew, Francis Crick, James Watson, and A.F. Huxley. It was at the Cavendish Laboratory that Francis Crick and James Watson discovered the structure of the DNA molecule.

Molecular biology gained a haven when a new laboratory was built and dedicated in 1962 with the support of the Medical Research Council. It attracted researchers such as Frederick Sanger, Aaron Klug, and César Milstein. Max Perutz has told of how he strove to create an environment that promoted communication:

"Experience had taught me that laboratories often fail because their scientists never talk to each other. To stimulate the exchange of ideas, we built a canteen where people can chat at morning coffee, lunch and tea. It was managed for over twenty years by my wife, Gisela, who

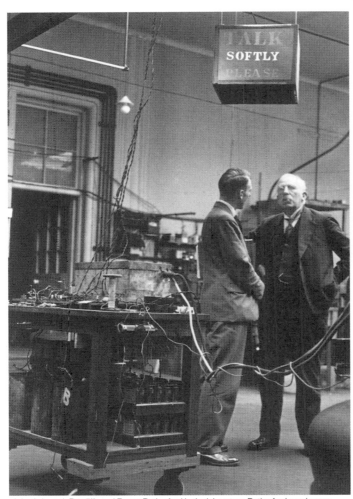

Francis Crick and James Watson in front of King's College Chapel.

Lawrence Bragg in his laboratory.

John Ashworth Ratcliffe and Ernest Rutherford in the laboratory. Rutherford was known for his loud voice. The sign above the two men reads "Talk softly please."

saw to it that the food was good and that it was a place where people would make friends. Scientific instruments were to be shared, rather than being jealously guarded as people's private property; this saved money and also forced people to talk to each other. When funds ran short during the building of the lab, I suggested that money could be saved by leaving all doors without locks to symbolize the absence of secrets."

Yet Perutz does not believe that creative environments can be organized into being. Creativity originates in the talents of the individual. "Well-run laboratories can foster it, but hierarchical organization, inflexible bureaucratic rules, and mountains of futile paperwork can kill it." According to Perutz, discoveries cannot be planned; they show up by themselves, in unexpected places.

Eagerness for discovery and the joy of work thrive at Cambridge. But as has been pointed out, the competition is also extreme. Why would anyone want to work in such an environment?

The answer to this question lies perhaps in the many creative people. In the environment of Cambridge's colleges they find opportunity to associate with one another during lunch, over coffee, or at the pub after work. Piotr Kapitsa remembered his time in Cambridge in the 1920s and 1930s:

"When I worked in England, I found that the most interesting conversations on the throbbing problems of science were held at college dinners. We used to discuss there problems that embraced many areas of science at one and the same time, and this was the best way of broadening our horizon and of comprehending the current significance of this or that scientific thought."

Similar comments can be heard about present day Cambridge. "In Cambridge I can meet experts from every possible discipline," says one Australian poet active there today. "At dinner I discuss the latest discoveries in astronomy with one of England's leading physicists, next morning I arrange a poetry reading with a well known Kenyan author. Each new meeting inspires my creativity. I would not want to work anywhere else in the world."

Through a large antenna system, of which this wire was a small part, signals from space were transmitted to the radio astronomers in Cambridge. The antenna system was designed and constructed in the 1960s by a team led by astrophysicist Antony Hewish, who is in the photograph at the left.

At the top of the opposite page, a chart where a young graduate student, Jocelyn Bell, observed a source of radiation that had not previously been registered. The curve in the chart below, which was registered some time later, showed that the radiation varied periodically. There was no explanation for the phenomenon and the researchers wondered if it was caused by perturbations. Jokingly, Jocelyn Bell called the radiation LGM—"Little Green Men." However, further research verified that a new type of star had been discovered—a pulsar.

For the discovery of pulsars, Antony Hewish was awarded the Nobel Prize in physics for 1974, which was shared with his colleague Martin Ryle. A controversy broke out in which several people argued that Jocelyn Bell should have been awarded a share of the prize. Jocelyn Bell herself has had a very humble attitude and has said that she does not think she should have been awarded a share of the prize. She has stressed that the discovery to some extent had to do with luck and that the discovery she made as a young graduate student was not in itself worthy of a Nobel Prize.

Nevertheless, the case illustrates some difficult and not unusual issues in contemporary science. What is the role of chance in science? Who should get credit for the results derived in modern science, where a lot of the work is performed in large teams with collaborators in various positions? Is it more difficult for young women to assert themselves than it is for men in similar positions?

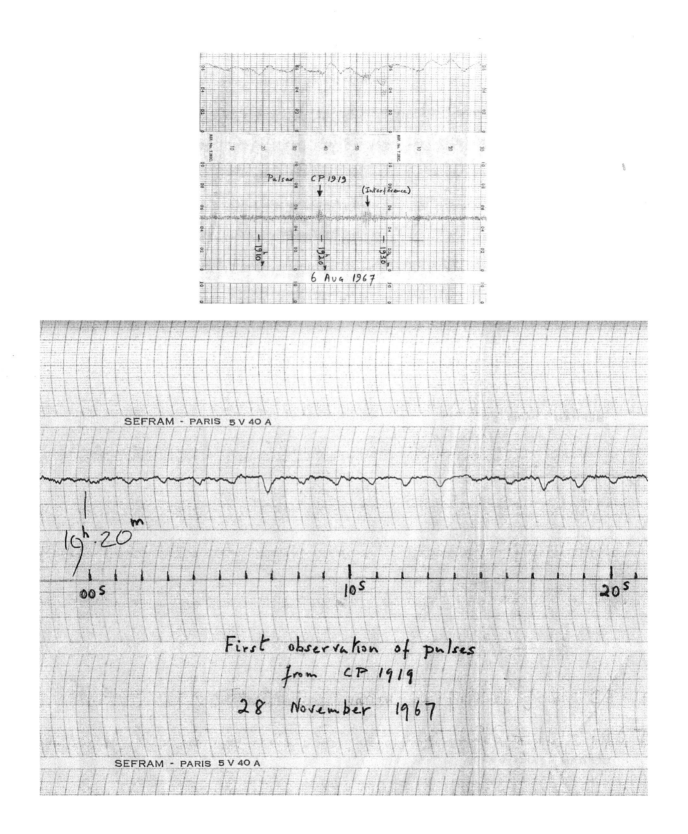

Pulsar CP 1919

(Interférence)

1910ʰ 1920ʰ 1930ʰ

6 Aug 1967

SEFRAM - PARIS 5 V 40 A

10ʰ.20ᵐ

00ˢ   10ˢ   20ˢ

First observation of pulses
from CP 1919
28 November 1967

SEFRAM - PARIS 5 V 40 A

In his painting *The Reading* the Belgian artist Theo van Rysselberghe has depicted the meeting between Belgian and French authors in Paris around 1900. Standing from left: Felix Feneon, Henri Gheon. Sitting from left: Feliz Le Dantec, Emile Verhaeren, Francis Viele-Griffen, Henri-Edmond Cross, André Gide, and Maurice Maeterlinck; the last two were future Nobel laureates.

Cafe des Deux Magots, one of Paris's most famous cafés.

Rendezvous for exiles

Paris

The Paris of literature and art carries instant associations for many. The clinking of china and glass. Cafés and bistros for conversation, thinking, and writing. Galleries and salons where new directions are presented and discussed.

Paris has held its central role for centuries, but the years between the two World Wars of the 1900s stand out as a period of especially intense flowering. Between the wars, Paris became the great place of exile for artists, bohemians, and political refugees. The city was alive with artistic creativity. These years saw an explosion of vitality, artistic experimentation, and seminal meetings between radical artists and their different genres that is perhaps still unequalled. Writers, painters, sculptors, choreographers, and composers from all over the world met here.

Demarcations between the various art forms seemed to have been erased. Different disciplines were united in new constellations. Jean Cocteau, one of the most praised artists of the 1920s, was not only an author, dramatist, and painter. He was also a jazz pianist, actor, film director, choreographer, and composer, and he showed himself to be a virtuoso in each of these areas. Cocteau became a symbol for the spirit of experimentation and the attitude of revolt that prevailed. Various new movements collided with one another, were born, and died in rapid succession. André Breton, who had just left the Dada movement, penned the first surrealist manifesto. Braque and Picasso, who had recently introduced cubism, were already on their way into new areas of artistic research. Composers such as Satie were inspired by painters and poets. Man Ray and Marcel Duchamps experimented

Coffee cup from La Coupole, one of the meeting places in Paris.

with film, as did Fernand Léger, who made the film *Ballet mécanique*. Russian ballet master Serge Diaghilev cooperated with new artists and composers.

One environment that became something of a microcosm of the entire Paris scene was the bookstore Shakespeare and Company. American Sylvia Beach had come to Paris in 1916 to study French poetry. A small advertisement led her to Adrienne Monnier's bookstore, and with her support, Beach started her bookstore Shakespeare and Company on Rue de l'Odeon on November 19, 1919. "The news of my bookshop, to my surprise, soon spread all over the United States, and it was the first thing the pilgrims looked up in Paris. They were all customers at Shakespeare and Company, which many of them looked upon as their club."

Sylvia Beach's bookstore became more than just a meeting place for expatriates; it functioned as a post office, work space for mobile magazine editors, and a borrowing library. A number of French writers curious about English-language literature also came here to meet their

Ernest Hemingway, in the side-car, at the Arch of Triumph in Paris.

Henri Bergson at his desk.

The publishing house and bookshop Shakespeare and Company at Rue l'Odéon was a meeting place for writers, artists and others in Paris between the world wars. The photograph depicts Myrsine and Hélène Moschos, Sylvia Beach, and Ernest Hemingway outside the bookshop in 1928.

André Gide.

colleagues. One of the first customers to sign his name in the library's register was André Gide. Eventually Beach also founded a publishing house, and it was here that James Joyce was finally able to find a publisher for his novel *Odysseus*.

Another regular at Shakespeare and Company was author Gertrude Stein, who had moved to Paris in 1907. Her experimental prose was inspired by the modern editing techniques of film, and by French philosopher Henri Bergson. In Paris, she came to have great influence as a source of inspiration and free-speaking critic to the circle of artists and writers she gathered on Rue de Fleuris. Her apartment functioned as a salon of old. Gertrude Stein spent most of her money on art, and on her walls hung works by Picasso, Braque, Juan Gris, and the other avant garde artists. Many authors, among them Ernest Hem-

ingway, have attested to the strong impression these paintings made, and how fascinating it was to listen to the discussions and theories concerning the new art.

Perhaps Hemingway has best depicted the atmosphere in Paris at this time. In *A Moveable Feast* he writes about the prerequisites the city had for developing creative artists. Crowded conditions, hunger, and relative poverty made these artists dependent on good friends and colleagues who crossed paths at cafés, galleries, and museums.

At the core of this movement was the circle of young journalists whom Gertrude Stein called "the lost generation"—"une génération perdue"—those who had participated in the war and had stayed in Paris: Ernest Hemingway, John Dos Passos, Malcom Crowley, and Dashiell Hammett. Others included Sherwood Anderson,

Robert Pinget, Samuel Beckett, and Claude Simon in a street in Paris, 1959.

Simone de Beauvoir and Jean-Paul Sartre at a rehearsal of Sartre's play *Nekrassov* at the Théâtre Antoine in 1955.

Albert Camus, in mirror, at a Parisian restaurant in 1957.

Ezra Pound, F. Scott Fitzgerald, and Henry Miller. They had fled the provincialism, racist views, alcohol prohibition, and middle-class ideals of their homeland. Paris became their asylum, and the bohemian lifestyle stimulated a new cosmopolitan attitude. Low prices and a favorable exchange on the dollar made it possible for them to devote themselves to the exciting restaurant and café scene. Most of the writers and intellectuals not only socialized but also did their work in these public places.

Toward the end of the 1920s, Samuel Beckett also came to Paris, and even he soon ended up in the circle surrounding Joyce and Sylvia Beach.

The years between the wars stands out as a golden age in the cultural life of Paris. Even after WWII, the city remained a fountain of creativity. With Jean-Paul Sartre and Albert Camus as its representatives, existentialism broke forth as a new philosophical and literary movement.

Paris retains its position as one of the world's most fascinating and stimulating cities. For Hemingway, Paris was a city to return to, as we see in *A Moveable Feast*, when he looked back on his life in the Paris of the 1920s:

"There is never any ending to Paris and the memory of each person who has lived in it differs from that of any other. We always return to it no matter who we were or how it was changed or with what difficulties, or ease, it could be reached. Paris was always worth it and you received return for whatever you brought to it. But this is how Paris was in the early days when we were very poor and very happy."

Young writers Shinzaburo Iketani, Yoichi Nakagawa, Kinsaku Ishihama, Yasunari Kawabata, and Tadao Suga belonged to a circle centered around the journal *Bungei Jidai* in the late 1920s.

Yasushi Inoue, Yasunari Kawabata, and Yukio Mishima talking in the bar Bunshun.

Blossoms among the ruins

Tokyo

Clean, spare beauty, yet with a sense of great drama—this is how we usually think of Japanese art and literature. Japanese culture has ancient roots, and its literature is rich. But modern Japan, too, has a long assemblage of outstanding authors.

European literary modernism was introduced as early as the 1920s in Japan. After WWII came a groundswell of new Japanese literature. Many authors popular before the war were inactive during it, only to achieve the height of their literary careers after the war's end. A younger generation of writers who had grown up during the war had been unable to practice their craft, due not least of all to the censure enforced by the military regime. Even they now got their first chance to write in earnest.

By tradition, literary journals have been an important forum for a literary career in Japan, even more so than in Europe. A whole array of new journals appeared on the market at the same time as the older journals put on hold during the war re-appeared. However, the difficulties were great. The entire Japanese printing industry had been decimated by American aerial bombing, and there was a severe paper shortage. Many of these journals did not survive beyond two or three issues.

The central figure in this movement was Yasunari Kawabata. During the final phase of the war, he and several friends started a library in Kamakura outside Tokyo. After the war, it was transformed into a publishing house, with Kawabata as its creative leader. A literary magazine, *Ningen*, was begun. Among others, Yukio Mishima published one of his early short stories one year after the war. Kawabata was always on the lookout for new talents, and

Kawabata playing shogi with Ri'ichi Yokomitsu in 1937.

Mishima, barely twenty years old at the time, became one of his brightest young stars. Kawabata himself entered a new period as an author, and in 1948 he was also elected chairman of Japan's PEN Club, a position in which he was intensely active. He worked tirelessly to invite foreign authors to the first international PEN meeting, held in Japan in 1957, at Tokyo and Kyoto. This was the first meaningful contact foreign intellectuals had had with modern Japan and its literature, and it led to the new Japanese authors being translated and introduced to Western readers in earnest.

This artistic exchange between East and West became even more intense after the end of the war, when Japan's relative isolation under the military regime was broken. Kobo Abe was clearly influenced by Franz Kafka, and that Kenzaburo Oe had read Sartre with care is obvious in his early novels, not least of all in *The Nightmare*.

The Café Museum, one of Vienna's famous cafés, designed by Adolf Loos in 1899. Elias Canetti has written a strange little story from a time when he used to go to the Café Museum. Among the other guests he noticed someone who strongly resembled the writer Karl Kraus—a legendary character in the intellectual sphere of Vienna for whom Canetti felt a strong admiration. Canetti observed the man every day during a year and a half—always in silence. This would prove to have a strong impact on Canetti's development. "Only later did I realize that this silent relationship brought about a cleavage. Little by little, my veneration detached itself from Karl Kraus and turned to his silent likeness. My psychological economy, in which veneration has always played a prominent part, was undergoing a profound change, all the more profound because it took place in silence."

Upheaval and regeneration

Vienna

The Viennese café—a place for creative contemplation as well as stimulating meetings and exchange of thoughts. Vienna is one of the best examples of the city as a workshop for creative processes.

This is especially true of the period 1880–1930, the time of the Hapsburg double monarchy's disintegration, WWI, and the birth and early years of the Austrian Republic. Creative achievements were made in many areas. Vienna was the workplace of composer Arnold Schönberg and Gustav Mahler; Sigmund Freud and Carl Gustav Jung, the founders of psychoanalysis; painters Gustav Klimt and Oskar Kokoschka; architects Otto Wagner and Adolf Loos; philosophers Otto Weininger and Ludwig Wittgenstein; and author and journalist Karl Kraus, a central figure. Author Elias Canetti spent most of his youth in Vienna.

Even Alfred Nobel sometimes visited Vienna, and Bertha von Suttner lived there for a time. Science blossomed in Vienna as well. Physicists Ludwig Boltzmann and Heinrich Hertz worked here, as did medical researchers Robert Bárány, Julius Wagner-Jauregg, Karl Landsteiner, and Konrad Lorenz, and economist Joseph Schumpeter. Physicists Erwin Schrödinger and Wolfgang Pauli, biochemist Max Perutz, and economist Friedrich von Hayek all grew up and studied in Vienna.

How can it be that a string of seemingly unrelated disciplines such as philosophy, scientific theory, economics, medicine, psychiatry, physics, mathematics, poetry, music, painting, architecture, theater, journalism, and political thinking underwent such remarkable renewals in the same time and place?

Elias Canetti reading his *Komödie der Eitelkeit*.

Some of the changes during this period were due to political circumstances. During the last years of the Hapsburg double monarchy, Vienna was like a pressure cooker. A nearly totalitarian regime and pervasive, rigid social conservatism limited the possibilities for social, political, economic, and cultural experimentation—yet

Chair designed for the Café Museum by Adolf Loos.

Elias Canetti with his cousin Mathilde Canetti in Vienna in 1928.

under the lid, things were boiling.

At the time of WWI, the pent-up spirit of experimentation came pouring forth. Old authorities disappeared and outdated institutions were dissolved. New and different modes of thought and style blossomed.

In this almost chaotic environment, many found their happiness. Yet many others did not fare well, and not all of the new ideas were good. Some would later show themselves to have fateful consequences for Europe—Vienna was one of the places where Nazism began.

Vienna's long traditions of learning provided the foundations for renewal. In art and science, Vienna's innovators were able to build upon long traditions and established, well developed competencies.

A key aspect of the city's role in encouraging creative processes was communication. The Danube was a major traffic artery between east and west. Over the plains just to the east, people and goods streamed between north and south. In the huge Austro-Hungarian Empire, Vienna held a unique position as a cultural, administra-

tive, and economic center. In cultural influence and as a powerhouse of thought, only Paris could compete with Vienna.

Vienna's population density was important to the city's function as a meeting place. Today we suppose that creative processes require lengthy specialization and that competence and creativity grow and develop best within narrow sectors. Such deeply rooted specialists existed in Vienna as well. Yet at the same time, communications functioned surprisingly well across disciplinary lines there. Comprehensive views as well as detailed technical information circulated in tightly woven networks between artists and scientists who met and conversed almost daily. The physical environment of Vienna was a strong contributing factor. Vienna's historical housing shortage further worsened between 1857 and 1910, when the city's population skyrocketed from 470,000 to just under 2 million. In this environment, Viennese café culture flourished. When people wanted to meet, they went to a café.

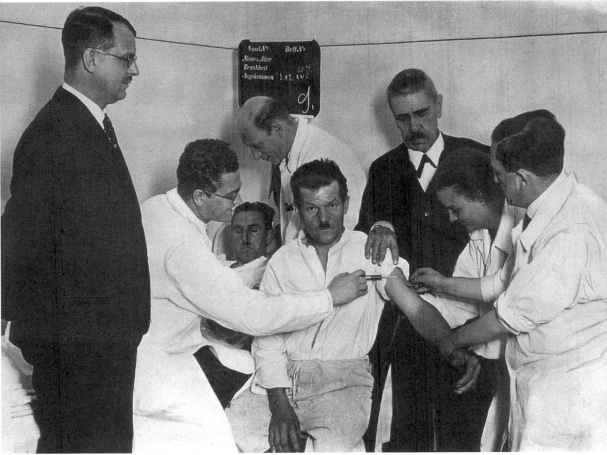

Psychiatrist Julius Wagner-Jauregg, third from the right, at a malaria inoculation. To alleviate or cure *paralysie générale*, a brain disease caused by syphilis, the patient was inoculated with malaria. The method is no longer used.

Karl Landsteiner, who discovered the blood types, lived and worked in Vienna before moving to New York in the 1930s.

The first Solvay Conference in 1911 gathered together many prominent physicists. Standing from the left: Robert Goldschmidt, Max Planck, Heinrich Rubens, Arnold Sommerfeld, Frederick Alexander Lindemann, Louis de Broglie, Martin Knudsen, Friedrich Hasenöhrl, L. Hostelet, Edouard Herzen, James Jeans, Ernest Rutherford, Heike Kamerlingh-Onnes, Albert Einstein, Paul Langevin. Sitting at the table from the left: Walther Nernst, Marcel Louis Brillouin, Ernest Solvay, Hendrik Antoon Lorentz, Emil Warburg, Jean Perrin, Wilhelm Wien, Marie Curie, Henri Poincaré.

The creative conference
The Solvay Conferences

Conferences and meetings are among the most important points of exchange for science. Although meetings are only temporary, they may have lasting results. It is not only the content of presentations and discussions that is important. They also provide an opportunity to make new contacts and lay the cornerstones for cooperation that will last long after the conference closes. Conferences are temporary, moveable environments of creativity.

Some of the most eminent conferences in the field of physics are the Solvay Conferences. They were initiated by Belgian chemist and industrial leader Ernest Solvay, who supported the sciences in various ways, including through the donation of funds to research institutes.

With the help of physical chemist Walter Nernst, Solvay organized the first Solvay Conference in 1911. At this meeting, some of the foremost physicists in Europe gathered to discuss the quantum hypothesis of physics. Each day, only several presentations were made, each of which was then discussed in detail.

This initial meeting was a scientific success and inspired Solvay to see to it that the conferences continued. The second Solvay Conference was held in 1913. After an interruption during WWI, five conferences were organized every third year between 1921 and 1933. These first seven conferences have become famous. This is true partly because they coincided with the breakthrough of quantum physics. The Solvay Conferences played an important role to a great extent because younger researchers were given the opportunity to present new discoveries and ideas and to discuss them with an older generation of physicists. Most of the founders of the new

Albert Einstein and Niels Bohr at the seventh Solvay Conference in 1933.

physics took part in the Solvay Conferences: Albert Einstein, Niels Bohr, Ernest Rutherford and many others. One physicist participated in seven of the first Solvay Conferences—Marie Curie.

After WWII, the Conferences were resumed in 1948, and have continued since then with a meeting approximately every third year. Today there are Solvay Conferences not only in physics but also in chemistry. Nonetheless, it is the first seven Solvay Conferences in physics that have become legendary in the history of science.

Mekong wheelchair manufactured at a workshop run by Tun
Channareth, an ICBL member. Tun Channareth lost both his legs
in a landmine accident.

Building shoe pyramids has been one of the campaign's methods of molding
public opinion. In the photograph, Tun Channareth, Man Sokherm, and Truk at a
shoe pyramid in Geneva in 1996.

A creative network

The ICBL

Is an environment necessarily confined to one geographical location, or can it be spread out and abstract? Can an environment be created using the telephone, telefax, and electronic mail?

The International Campaign to Ban Landmines—known by the abbreviation ICBL—consists of a vast group of organizations and people. Together they may be seen as an environment in which people work in different ways toward a common goal: to bring about a ban on landmines. In many countries around the world, huge quantities of landmines lie buried, posing a threat to innocent civilians and not least of all to playing children.

The ICBL was formed in 1992 when a handful of organizations joined forces to work for a ban. The campaign has succeeded in attracting a huge number of people from diverse backgrounds, and today it includes 1200 organizations in 80 countries. Member organizations are independent, and the loose structure of the ICBL has proven to be one of its strengths. The lack of central leadership and bureaucracy has strengthened the group's sense of involvement and belonging.

The ICBL uses the communication methods of the day. In the first years, members communicated by telefax. Over time, electronic mail and the Internet have become increasingly important.

When the ICBL began its work, few could conceive of the successes that would be achieved. Not even the most devoted participants dared believe that a few years would bring broad international support for a landmine ban.

A breakthrough occurred when Canada departed from the traditional diplomatic process. In October 1996,

Steve Goose, Jody Williams, and Mary Wareham working on responses to the draft of the Mine Ban Treaty during a conference in Oslo in September 1997.

Canada's Foreign Minister Lloyd Axworthy delivered a challenge calling for the negotiation of an international ban against landmines within one year. This put pressure on other nations, and the negotiations proceeded at record speed. In December 1997, representatives from 121 countries came to Ottawa to sign the agreement.

The ICBL's capacity to foster broad engagement at the "grass roots level" and to influence those in power is innovative. It may well serve as a model for future campaigns in the cause of world peace.

Cambodian children are educated to avoid landmines.

Mine clearing in Angola.

Monks march in Phnom Penh, Cambodia, in April 1996.

A woman gathering wood in Angola in 1997. Life goes on and the children need food, even if one leg is lost.

A landmine is detonated.

Explosives are placed at a landmine in order to detonate it.

Nobel Laureates 1901–2000

PHYSICS

1901 Wilhelm Conrad Röntgen
1902 Hendrik Antoon Lorentz and Pieter Zeeman
1903 Antoine Henri Becquerel, Pierre Curie, and Marie Sklodowska Curie
1904 Lord (John William Strutt) Rayleigh
1905 Philipp Eduard Anton von Lenard
1906 Joseph John Thomson
1907 Albert Abraham Michelson
1908 Gabriel Lippmann
1909 Guglielmo Marconi and Carl Ferdinand Braun
1910 Johannes Diderik van der Waals
1911 Wilhelm Wien
1912 Nils Gustaf Dalén
1913 Heike Kamerlingh-Onnes
1914 Max von Laue
1915 Sir William Henry Bragg and William Lawrence Bragg
1916 Prize not awarded
1917 Prize not awarded
1918 The prize for 1917: Charles Glover Barkla; The prize for 1918: Prize not awarded
1919 The prize for 1918: Max Karl Ernst Ludwig Planck; The prize for 1919: Johannes Stark
1920 Charles Edouard Guillaume
1921 Prize not awarded
1922 The prize for 1921: Albert Einstein; The prize for 1922: Niels Henrik David Bohr
1923 Robert Andrews Millikan
1924 Prize not awarded
1925 The prize for 1924: Karl Manne Georg Siegbahn
1926 The prize for 1925: James Franck and Gustav Ludwig Hertz; The prize for 1926: Jean Baptiste Perrin
1927 Arthur Holly Compton and Charles Thomson Rees Wilson
1928 Prize not awarded
1929 The prize for 1928: Owen Willans Richardson; The prize for 1929: Prince Louis-Victor Pierre Raymond de Broglie
1930 Sir Chandrasekhara Venkata Raman
1931 Prize not awarded
1932 Prize not awarded
1933 The prize for 1932: Werner Karl Heisenberg; The prize for 1933: Erwin Schrödinger and Paul Adrien Maurice Dirac
1934 Prize not awarded
1935 James Chadwick
1936 Victor Franz Hess and Carl David Anderson
1937 Clinton Joseph Davisson and George Paget Thomson
1938 Enrico Fermi
1939 Ernest Orlando Lawrence
1940 Prize not awarded
1941 Prize not awarded
1942 Prize not awarded
1943 Prize not awarded
1944 The prize for 1943: Otto Stern; The prize for 1944: Isidor Isaac Rabi
1945 Wolfgang Pauli
1946 Percy Williams Bridgman
1947 Sir Edward Victor Appleton
1948 Patrick Maynard Stuart Blackett
1949 Hideki Yukawa
1950 Cecil Frank Powell
1951 Sir John Douglas Cockcroft and Ernest Thomas Sinton Walton
1952 Felix Bloch and Edward Mills Purcell
1953 Frits (Frederik) Zernike
1954 Max Born and Walther Bothe
1955 Willis Eugene Lamb and Polykarp Kusch
1956 William Bradford Shockley, John Bardeen, and Walter Houser Brattain
1957 Chen Ning Yang and Tsung-Dao Lee
1958 Pavel Alekseyevich Cherenkov, Il'ja Mikhailovich Frank, and Igor Yergenyevich Tamm
1959 Emilio Gino Segrè and Owen Chamberlain
1960 Donald Arthur Glaser
1961 Robert Hofstadter and Rudolf Ludwig Mössbauer
1962 Lev Davidovich Landau
1963 Eugene Paul Wigner, Maria Goeppert-Mayer, and J. Hans D. Jensen
1964 Charles Hard Townes, Nicolay Gennadiyevich Basov, and Aleksandr Mikhailovich Prokhorov
1965 Sin-Itiro Tomonaga, Julian Schwinger, and Richard P. Feynman
1966 Alfred Kastler
1967 Hans Albrecht Bethe
1968 Luis Walter Alvarez
1969 Murray Gell-Mann
1970 Hannes Olof Gösta Alfvén and Louis Eugène Félix Néel
1971 Dennis Gabor
1972 John Bardeen, Leon Neil Cooper, and John Robert Schrieffer
1973 Leo Esaki, Ivar Giaever, and Brian David Josephson
1974 Sir Martin Ryle and Antony Hewish
1975 Aage Niels Bohr, Ben Roy Mottelson, and Leo James Rainwater
1976 Burton Richter and Samuel Chao Chung Ting
1977 Philip Warren Anderson, Sir Nevill Francis Mott, and John Hasbrouck van Vleck
1978 Pyotr Leonidovich Kapitsa, Arno Allan Penzias, and Robert Woodrow Wilson
1979 Sheldon Lee Glashow, Abdus Salam, and Steven Weinberg
1980 James Watson Cronin and Val Logsdon Fitch
1981 Nicolaas Bloembergen, Arthur Leonard Schawlow, and Kai M. Siegbahn
1982 Kenneth G. Wilson
1983 Subramanyan Chandrasekhar and William Alfred Fowler
1984 Carlo Rubbia and Simon Van der Meer
1985 Klaus von Klitzing
1986 Ernst Ruska, Gerd Binnig, and Heinrich Rohrer
1987 J. Georg Bednorz and K. Alexander Müller
1988 Leon M. Lederman, Melvin Schwartz, and Jack Steinberger
1989 Norman F. Ramsey, Hans G. Dehmelt, and Wolfgang Paul
1990 Jerome I. Friedman, Henry W. Kendall, and Richard E. Taylor
1991 Pierre-Gilles de Gennes
1992 Georges Charpak
1993 Russell A. Hulse and Joseph H. Taylor, Jr.
1994 Bertram N. Brockhouse and Clifford G. Shull
1995 Martin L. Perl and Frederick Reines
1996 David M. Lee, Douglas D. Osheroff, and Robert C. Richardson

1997 Steven Chu, Claude Cohen-Tannoudji, and William D. Phillips
1998 Robert B. Laughlin, Horst L. Störmer, and Daniel C. Tsui
1999 Gerardus ´t Hooft and Martinus J. G. Veltman
2000 Zhores I. Alferov, Herbert Kroemer, and Jack S. Kilby

CHEMISTRY

1901 Jacobus Henricus Van't Hoff
1902 Hermann Emil Fischer
1903 Svante August Arrhenius
1904 Sir William Ramsay
1905 Johann Friedrich Wilhelm Adolf von Baeyer
1906 Henri Moissan
1907 Eduard Buchner
1908 Ernest Rutherford
1909 Wilhelm Ostwald
1910 Otto Wallach
1911 Marie Curie, née Sklodowska
1912 Victor Grignard and Paul Sabatier
1913 Alfred Werner
1914 Prize not awarded
1915 The prize for 1914: Theodore William Richards The prize for 1915: Richard Martin Willstätter
1916 Prize not awarded
1917 Prize not awarded
1918 Prize not awarded
1919 The prize for 1918: Fritz Haber; The prize for 1919 Prize not awarded
1920 Prize not awarded
1921 The prize for 1920: Walther Hermann Nernst; The prize for 1921: Prize not awarded
1922 The prize for 1921: Frederick Soddy; The prize for 1922: Francis William Aston
1923 Fritz Pregl
1924 Prize not awarded
1925 Prize not awarded
1926 The prize for 1925: Richard Adolf Zsigmondy; The prize for 1926: The (Theodor) Svedberg
1927 Prize not awarded
1928 The prize for 1927: Heinrich Otto Wieland; The prize for 1928: Adolf Otto Reinhold Windaus
1929 Arthur Harden and Hans Karl August Simon von Euler-Chelpin
1930 Hans Fischer
1931 Carl Bosch and Friedrich Bergius
1932 Irving Langmuir
1933 Prize not awarded
1934 Harold Clayton Urey
1935 Frédéric Joliot and Irène Joliot-Curie
1936 Petrus (Peter) Josephus Wilhelmus Debye

1937 Walter Norman Haworth and Paul Karrer
1938 Prize not awarded
1939 The prize for 1938: Richard Kuhn The prize for 1939: Adolf Friedrich Johann Butenandt and Leopold Ruzicka
1940 Prize not awarded
1941 Prize not awarded
1942 Prize not awarded
1943 Prize not awarded
1944 The prize for 1943: George de Hevesy; The prize for 1944: Prize not awarded
1945 The prize for 1944: Otto Hahn; The prize for 1945: Artturi Ilmari Virtanen
1946 James Batcheller Sumner, John Howard Northrop, and Wendell Meredith Stanley
1947 Sir Robert Robinson
1948 Arne Wilhelm Kaurin Tiselius
1949 William Francis Giauque
1950 Otto Diels, Paul Hermann, and Kurt Alder
1951 Edwin Mattison McMillan, and Glenn Theodore Seaborg
1952 Archer John Porter Martin, and Richard Laurence Millington Synge
1953 Hermann Staudinger
1954 Linus Carl Pauling
1955 Vincent du Vigneaud
1956 Sir Cyril Norman Hinshelwood and Nikolay Nikolaevich Semenov
1957 Lord Alexander R. Todd
1958 Frederick Sanger
1959 Jaroslav Heyrovsky
1960 Willard Frank Libby
1961 Melvin Calvin
1962 Max Ferdinand Perutz and John Cowdery Kendrew
1963 Karl Ziegler and Giulio Natta
1964 Dorothy Crowfoot Hodgkin
1965 Robert Burns Woodward
1966 Robert S. Mulliken
1967 Manfred Eigen, Ronald George Wreyford Norrish, and George Porter
1968 Lars Onsager
1969 Derek H. R. Barton and Odd Hassel
1970 Luis F. Leloir
1971 Gerhard Herzberg
1972 Christian B. Anfinsen, Stanford Moore, and William H. Stein
1973 Ernst Otto Fischer and Geoffrey Wilkinson
1974 Paul J. Flory
1975 John Warcup Cornforth and Vladimir Prelog
1976 William N. Lipscomb
1977 Ilya Prigogine

1978 Peter D. Mitchell
1979 Herbert C. Brown and Georg Wittig
1980 Paul Berg, Walter Gilbert, and Frederick Sanger
1981 Kenichi Fukui and Roald Hoffmann
1982 Aaron Klug
1983 Henry Taube
1984 Robert Bruce Merrifield
1985 Herbert A. Hauptman and Jerome Karle
1986 Dudley R. Herschbach, Yuan T. Lee, and John C. Polanyi
1987 Donald J. Cram, Jean-Marie Lehn, and Charles J. Pedersen
1988 Johann Deisenhofer Robert Huber and Hartmut Michel
1989 Sidney Altman and Thomas R. Cech
1990 Elias James Corey
1991 Richard R. Ernst
1992 Rudolph A. Marcus
1993 Kary B. Mullis and Michael Smith
1994 George A. Olah
1995 Paul J. Crutzen, Mario J. Molina, and F. Sherwood Rowland
1996 Robert F. Curl Jr., Sir Harold W. Kroto, and Richard E. Smalley
1997 Paul D. Boyer, John E. Walker, and Jens C. Skou
1998 Walter Kohn and John A. Pople
1999 Ahmed H. Zewail
2000 Alan J. Heeeger, Alan G MacDiarmid, and Hideki Shirakawa

PHYSIOLOGY OR MEDICINE

1901 Emil Adolf von Behring
1902 Ronald Ross
1903 Niels Ryberg Finsen
1904 Ivan Petrovich Pavlov
1905 Robert Koch
1906 Camillo Golgi and Santiago Ramón y Cajal
1907 Charles Louis Alphonse Laveran
1908 Ilya Ilyich Mechnikov and Paul Ehrlich
1909 Emil Theodor Kocher
1910 Albrecht Kossel
1911 Allvar Gullstrand
1912 Alexis Carrel
1913 Charles Robert Richet
1914 Robert Bárány
1915 Prize not awarded
1916 Prize not awarded
1917 Prize not awarded
1918 Prize not awarded
1919 Prize not awarded
1920 The prize for 1919: Jules Bordet; The prize for 1920: Schack August Steenberg Krogh
1921 Prize not awarded
1922 Prize not awarded

1923 The prize for 1922: Archibald Vivian Hill and Otto Fritz Meyerhof; The prize for 1923: Frederick Grant Banting and John James Richard Macleod

1924 Willem Einthoven

1925 Prize not awarded

1926 Prize not awarded

1927 The prize for 1926: Johannes Andreas Grib Fibiger; The prize for 1927: Julius Wagner-Jauregg

1928 Charles Jules Henri Nicolle

1929 Christiaan Eijkman and Sir Frederick Gowland Hopkins

1930 Karl Landsteiner

1931 Otto Heinrich Warburg

1932 Sir Charles Scott Sherrington and Edgar Douglas Adrian

1933 Thomas Hunt Morgan

1934 George Hoyt Whipple, George Richards Minot, and William Parry Murphy

1935 Hans Spemann

1936 Sir Henry Hallett Dale and Otto Loewi

1937 Albert von Szent-Györgyi Nagyrapolt

1938 Prize not awarded

1939 The prize for 1938: Corneille Jean François Heymans; The prize for 1939: Gerhard Domagk

1940 Prize not awarded

1941 Prize not awarded

1942 Prize not awarded

1943 Prize not awarded

1944 The prize for 1943: Henrik Carl Peter Dam and Edward Adelbert Doisy; The prize for 1944: Joseph Erlanger and Herbert Spencer Gasser

1945 Sir Alexander Fleming, Ernst Boris Chain, and Sir Howard Walter Florey

1946 Hermann Joseph Muller

1947 Carl Ferdinand Cori, Gerty Theresa Cori, and Bernardo Alberto Houssay

1948 Paul Hermann Müller

1949 Walter Rudolf Hess and Antonio Caetano de Abreu Freire Egas Moniz

1950 Edward Calvin Kendall, Tadeus Reichstein, and Philip Showalter Hench

1951 Max Theiler

1952 Selman Abraham Waksman

1953 Hans Adolf Krebs and Fritz Albert Lipmann

1954 John Franklin Enders Thomas Huckle Weller and Frederick Chapman Robbins

1955 Axel Hugo Theodor Theorell

1956 André Frédéric Cournand, Werner Forssmann, and Dickinson W. Richards

1957 Daniel Bovet

1958 George Wells Beadle, Edward Lawrie Tatum, and Joshua Lederberg

1959 Severo Ochoa and Arthur Kornberg

1960 Sir Frank Macfarlane Burnet, and Peter Brian Medawar

1961 Georg von Békésy

1962 Francis Harry Compton Crick, James Dewey Watson, and Maurice Hugh Frederick Wilkins

1963 Sir John Carew Eccles, Alan Lloyd Hodgkin, and Andrew Fielding Huxley

1964 Konrad Bloch and Feodor Lynen

1965 François Jacob, André Lwoff, and Jacques Monod

1966 Peyton Rous and Charles Brenton Huggins

1967 Ragnar Granit, Haldan Keffer Hartline, and George Wald

1968 Robert W. Holley, Har Gobind Khorana, and Marshall W. Nirenberg

1969 Max Delbrück, Alfred D. Hershey, and Salvador E. Luria

1970 Sir Bernard Katz, Ulf von Euler, and Julius Axelrod

1971 Earl W. Sutherland, Jr.

1972 Gerald M. Edelman and Rodney R. Porter

1973 Karl von Frisch, Konrad Lorenz, and Nikolaas Tinbergen

1974 Albert Claude, Christian de Duve, and George E. Palade

1975 David Baltimore, Renato Dulbecco, and Howard Martin Temin

1976 Baruch S. Blumberg and D. Carleton Gajdusek

1977 Roger Guillemin, Andrew V. Schally, and Rosalyn Yalow

1978 Werner Arber, Daniel Nathans, and Hamilton O. Smith

1979 Allan M. Cormack and Godfrey N. Hounsfield

1980 Baruj Benacerraf, Jean Dausset, and George D. Snell

1981 Roger W. Sperry, David H. Hubel, and Torsten N. Wiesel

1982 Sune K. Bergström, Bengt I. Samuelsson, and John R. Vane

1983 Barbara McClintock

1984 Niels K. Jerne, Georges J. F. Köhler, and César Milstein

1985 Michael S. Brown and Joseph L. Goldstein

1986 Stanley Cohen and Rita Levi-Montalcini

1987 Susumu Tonegawa

1988 Sir James W. Black, Gertrude B. Elion, and George H. Hitchings

1989 J. Michael Bishop and Harold E. Varmus

1990 Joseph E. Murray and E. Donnall Thomas

1991 Erwin Neher and Bert Sakmann

1992 Edmond H. Fischer and Edwin G. Krebs

1993 Richard J. Roberts and Phillip A. Sharp

1994 Alfred G. Gilman and Martin Rodbell

1995 Edward B. Lewis, Christiane Nüsslein-Volhard, and Eric F. Wieschaus

1996 Peter C. Doherty and Rolf M. Zinkernagel

1997 Stanley B. Prusiner

1998 Robert F. Furchgott, Louis J. Ignarro, and Ferid Murad

1999 Günter Blobel

2000 Arvid Carlsson, Paul Greengard, and Eric Kandel

LITERATURE

1901 Sully Prudhomme

1902 Christian Matthias Theodor Mommsen

1903 Bjørnstjerne Martinus Bjørnson

1904 Frédéric Mistral and José Echegaray Y Eizaguirre

1905 Henryk Sienkiewicz

1906 Giosuè Carducci

1907 Rudyard Kipling

1908 Rudolf Christoph Eucken

1909 Selma Ottilia Lovisa Lagerlöf

1910 Paul Johann Ludwig Heyse

1911 Count Maurice (Mooris) Polidore Marie Bernhard Maeterlinck

1912 Gerhart Johann Robert Hauptmann

1913 Rabindranath Tagore

1914 Prize not awarded

1915 Prize not awarded

1916 The prize for 1915: Romain Rolland; The prize for 1916: Carl Gustaf Verner von Heidenstam

1917 Karl Adolph Gjellerup and Henrik Pontoppidan

1918 Prize not awarded

1919 Prize not awarded

1920 The prize for 1919: Carl Friedrich Georg Spitteler; The prize for 1920: Knut Pedersen Hamsun

1921 Anatole France

1922 Jacinto Benavente

1923 William Butler Yeats

1924 Wladyslaw Stanislaw Reymont

1925 Prize not awarded

1926 The prize for 1925: George Bernard Shaw; The prize for 1926: Prize not awarded

1927 The prize for 1926: Grazia Deledda The prize for 1927: Prize not awarded

1928 The prize for 1927: Henri Bergson; The prize for 1928: Sigrid Undset

1929 Thomas Mann

1930 Sinclair Lewis

1931 Erik Axel Karlfeldt

1932 John Galsworthy

1933 Ivan Alekseyevich Bunin

1934 Luigi Pirandello

1935 Prize not awarded

1936 Eugene Gladstone O'Neill

1937 Roger Martin du Gard

1938 Pearl Buck

1939 Frans Eemil Sillanpää

1940 Prize not awarded

1941 Prize not awarded

1942 Prize not awarded

1943 Prize not awarded

1944 Johannes Vilhelm Jensen

1945 Gabriela Mistral

1946 Hermann Hesse

1947 André Paul Guillaume Gide

1948 Thomas Stearns Eliot

1949 Prize not awarded

1950 The prize for 1949: William Faulkner The prize for 1950: Earl (Bertrand Arthur William) Russell

1951 Pär Fabian Lagerkvist

1952 François Mauriac

1953 Sir Winston Leonard Spencer Churchill

1954 Ernest Miller Hemingway

1955 Halldór Kiljan Laxness

1956 Juan Ramón Jiménez

1957 Albert Camus

1958 Boris Leonidovich Pasternak (Accepted first, later caused by the authorities of his country to decline the prize.)

1959 Salvatore Quasimodo

1960 Saint-John Perse

1961 Ivo Andric

1962 John Steinbeck

1963 Giorgos Seferis

1964 Jean-Paul Sartre (Declined the prize.)

1965 Michail Aleksandrovich Sholokhov

1966 Shmuel Yosef Agnon and Nelly Sachs

1967 Miguel Angel Asturias

1968 Yasunari Kawabata

1969 Samuel Beckett

1970 Aleksandr Isaevich Solzhenitsyn

1971 Pablo Neruda

1972 Heinrich Böll

1973 Patrick White

1974 Eyvind Johnson and Harry Martinson

1975 Eugenio Montale

1976 Saul Bellow

1977 Vicente Aleixandre

1978 Isaac Bashevis Singer

1979 Odysseus Elytis

1980 Czeslaw Milosz

1981 Elias Canetti

1982 Gabriel García Márquez

1983 William Golding

1984 Jaroslav Seifert

1985 Claude Simon

1986 Wole Soyinka

1987 Joseph Brodsky

1988 Naguib Mahfouz

1989 Camilo José Cela

1990 Octavio Paz

1991 Nadine Gordimer

1992 Derek Walcott

1993 Toni Morrison

1994 Kenzaburo Oe

1995 Seamus Heaney

1996 Wislawa Szymborska

1997 Dario Fo

1998 José Saramago

1999 Günter Grass

2000 Gao Xingjian

PEACE

1901 Jean Henri Dunant and Frédéric Passy

1902 Élie Ducommun and Charles Albert Gobat

1903 William Randal Cremer

1904 Institute Of International Law

1905 Baronessan Bertha Sophie Felicita von Suttner

1906 Theodore Roosevelt

1907 Ernesto Teodoro Moneta and Louis Renault

1908 Klas Pontus Arnoldson and Fredrik Bajer

1909 Auguste Marie François Beernaert and Baron Paul Henri Benjamin Balluet d'Estournelle de Constant

1910 Permanent International Peace Bureau

1911 Tobias Michael Carel Asser and Alfred Hermann Fried

1912 Prize not awarded

1913 The prize for 1912: Elihu Root; The prize for 1913: Henri La Fontaine

1914 Prize not awarded

1915 Prize not awarded

1916 Prize not awarded

1917 International Committee of the Red Cross

1918 Prize not awarded

1919 Prize not awarded

1920 The prize for 1919: Thomas Woodrow Wilson; The prize for 1920: Léon Victor Auguste Bourgeois

1921 Karl Hjalmar Branting and Christian Lous Lange

1922 Fridtjof Nansen

1923 Prize not awarded

1924 Prize not awarded

1925 Prize not awarded

1926 The prize for 1925: Sir Austen Chamberlain and Charles Gates Dawes; The prize for 1926: Aristide Briand and Gustav Stresemann

1927 Ferdinand Buisson and Ludwig Quidde

1928 Prize not awarded

1929 Prize not awarded

1930 The prize for 1929: Frank Billings Kellogg; The prize for 1930: Lars Olof Nathan (Jonathan) Söderblom

1931 Jane Addams and Nicholas Murray Butler

1932 Prize not awarded

1933 Prize not awarded

1934 The prize for 1933: Sir Norman Angell (Ralph Lane); The prize for 1934: Arthur Henderson

1935 Prize not awarded

1936 The prize for 1935: Carl von Ossietzky; The prize for 1936: Carlos Saavedra Lamas

1937 Viscount Cecil of Chelwood (Lord Edgar Algernon Robert Gascoyne Cecil)

1938 Nansen International Office for Refugees

1939 Prize not awarded

1940 Prize not awarded

1941 Prize not awarded

1942 Prize not awarded

1943 Prize not awarded

1944 Prize not awarded

1945 The prize for 1944: International Committee of the Red Cross; The prize for 1945: Cordell Hull

1946 Emily Greene Balch and John Raleigh Mott

1947 The Friends Service Council (The Quakers) and The American Friends Service Committee (the Quakers)

1948 Prize not awarded

1949 Lord (John) Boyd Orr of Brechin

1950 Ralph Bunche

1951 Léon Jouhaux

1952 Prize not awarded

1953 The prize for 1952: Albert Schweitzer; The prize for 1953: George Catlett Marshall

1954 Prize not awarded

1955 The prize for 1954: Office of the United Nations High Commissioner for Refugees; The prize for 1955: Prize not awarded

1956 Prize not awarded

1957 Lester Bowles Pearson

1958 Georges Pire

1959 Philip J. Noel-Baker

1960 Prize not awarded

1961 The prize for 1960: Albert John Lutuli; The prize for 1961: Dag Hjalmar Agne Carl Hammarskjöld

1962 Prize not awarded

1963 The prize for 1962: Linus Carl Pauling; The prize for 1963: International Committee of the Red Cross and League of Red Cross Societies

1964 Martin Luther King, Jr.

1965 United Nations Children's Fund (UNICEF)

1966 Prize not awarded

1967 Prize not awarded

1968 René Cassin

1969 International Labour Organization

1970 Norman Borlaug

1971 Willy Brandt

1972 Prize not awarded

1973 Henry A. Kissinger and Le Duc Tho (Declined the prize.)

1974 Sean MacBride and Eisaku Sato

1975 Andrei Dmitrievich Sakharov

1976 Prize not awarded

1977 The prize for 1976: Betty Williams and Mairead Corrigan; The prize for 1977: Amnesty International

1978 Mohamed Anwar el Sadat and Menachem Begin

1979 Mother Teresa

1980 Adolfo Perez Esquivel

1981 Office of the United Nations High Commissioner for Refugees

1982 Alva Myrdal and Alfonso García Robles

1983 Lech Walesa

1984 Desmond Mpilo Tutu

1985 International Physicians for the Prevention of Nuclear War Inc.

1986 Elie Wiesel

1987 Oscar Arias Sanchez

1988 The United Nations Peace-keeping Forces

1989 The 14th Dalai Lama (Tenzin Gyatso)

1990 Mikhail Sergeyevich Gorbachev

1991 Aung San Suu Kyi

1992 Rigoberta Menchú Tum

1993 Nelson Mandela and Frederik Willem de Klerk

1994 Yasser Arafat, Shimon Peres and Yitzhak Rabin

1995 Joseph Rotblat and Pugwash Conferences On Science And World Affairs

1996 Carlos Filipe Ximenes Belo and José Ramos-Horta

1997 International Campaign to Ban Landmines (ICBL) and Jody Williams

1998 John Hume and David Trimble

1999 Doctors without Borders

2000 Kim Dae-jung

ECONOMIC SCIENCES

1969 Ragnar Frisch and Jan Tinbergen

1970 Paul A. Samuelson

1971 Simon Kuznets

1972 John R. Hicks and Kenneth J. Arrow

1973 Wassily Leontief

1974 Gunnar Myrdal and Friedrich August von Hayek

1975 Leonid Vitaliyevich Kantorovich and Tjalling C. Koopmans

1976 Milton Friedman

1977 Bertil Ohlin and James E. Meade

1978 Herbert A. Simon

1979 Theodore W. Schultz and Arthur Lewis

1980 Lawrence R. Klein

1981 James Tobin

1982 George J. Stigler

1983 Gerard Debreu

1984 Richard Stone

1985 Franco Modigliani

1986 James M. Buchanan, Jr.

1987 Robert M. Solow

1988 Maurice Allais

1989 Trygve Haavelmo

1990 Harry M. Markowitz, Merton H. Miller, and William F. Sharpe

1991 Ronald H. Coase

1992 Gary S. Becker

1993 Robert W. Fogel and Douglass C. North

1994 John C. Harsanyi, John F. Nash, and Reinhard Selten

1995 Robert E. Lucas, Jr.

1996 James A. Mirrlees and William Vickrey

1997 Robert C. Merton and Myron S. Scholes

1998 Amartya Sen

1999 Robert A. Mundell

2000 James J. Heckman and Daniel McFadden

References

INTRODUCTION (PP. 11–13)
Wole Soyinka, speech in *Les Prix Nobel* 1986.
Wole Soyinka, *Early Poems* (New York, 1998).

ALFRED NOBEL AND HIS TIMES (P. 15-25)
Communiqués from Anders Ekström, Tore Frängsmyr, Marika Hedin, Anders Lundgren written for this exhibition project.
Erik Bergengren, *Alfred Nobel* (1960; London, 1962).

THE NOBEL SYSTEM (P. 27-35)
Ragnar Sohlman, *The legacy of Alfred Nobel: The story behind the Nobel prizes* (1950; London, 1983).

INDIVIDUAL CREATIVITY (P. 39)
Communiqués from Ulrika Björkstén, Gudmund Smith, and Jan Nolin written for this exhibition project.

MARIE CURIE (P. 41)
Communiqué from Ulrika Björkstén written for this exhibition project.
Soraya Boudia, "Marie Curie: Scientific entrepeneur," *Physics world*, December 1998, 35-39.
Nanny Fröman, "Marie and Pierre Curie and the Discovery of Polonium and Radium," http://www.nobel.se/physics/articles/curie/index.html

SAMUEL BECKETT (P. 45)
Communiqué from Magnus Jacobsson written for this exhibition project.
James Knowlson, *Damned to Fame: The life of Samuel Beckett* (London, 1996).

THE DALAI LAMA (P. 47)
Irwin Abrams, *The Nobel Peace Prize and the Laureates: An Illustrated Biographical History, 1901–1987* (Boston, 1998).

AMARTYA SEN (P. 49)
Communiqué from Marika Hedin written for this exhibition project.

BORIS PASTERNAK (P. 51)
Communiqués from Nina Burton and Anna Ljunggren written for this exhibition project.

LINUS PAULING (P. 55)
Irwin Abrams, *The Nobel Peace Prize and the Laureates: An Illustrated Biographical History, 1901–1987* (Boston, 1998).

AHMED ZEWAIL (P. 59)
Ahmed Zewail, autobiography in *Les Prix Nobel* 1999 (Stockholm, 2000).

WERNER FORSSMANN (P. 61)
Werner Forssmann, *Experiments on myself: Memoirs of a Surgeon in Germany* (New York, 1974).

BARBARA MC CLINTOCK (P. 63)
Communiqué from Monika Starendal written for this exhibition project.
Nina Fedoroff & David Botstein, *The Dynamic Genome: Barbara McClintock's ideas in the century of genetics* (Cold Spring Harbor, 1992).
Evelyn Fox Keller, *A Feeling for the Organism: The Life and Work of Barbara McClintock* (New York, 1983).
Howard Green, "In Memoriam—Barbara McClintock," http://www.nobel.se/medicine/articles/green/index.html.

NELLY SACHS (P. 67)
Communiqué from Nina Burton written for this exhibition project.

AUNG SAN SUU KYI (P. 69)
Aung San Suu Kyi, *Freedom from Fear* (London, 1991, revised ed., 1995).

YASUNARI KAWABATA (P. 71)
Communiqué from Nina Burton written for this exhibition project.

DAG HAMMARSKJÖLD (P. 73)
Irwin Abrams, *The Nobel Peace Prize and the Laureates: An Illustrated Biographical History, 1901–1987* (Boston, 1998).
Dag Hammarskjöld, *Markings* (New York, 1964).
Brian Urquhart, *Hammarskjold* (New York, 1972).

HIDEKI YUKAWA (P. 77)
Communiqué from Anders Bárány written for this exhibition project.
Hideki Yukawa, *Tabibito: the traveler* (Singapore, 1982).

ERNEST HEMINGWAY (P. 81)
Communiqué from Nina Burton written for this exhibition project.
Ernest Hemingway, speech in *Les Prix Nobel 1954* (Stockholm 1955).

ISAAC BASHEVIS SINGER (P. 83)
Communiqué from Stephen Farran-Lee written for this exhibition project.
Isaac Bashevis Singer, *Lost in America* (New York, 1981).
Isaac Bashevis Singer & Richard Burgin, *Conversations with Isaac Bashevis Singer* (Garden City, NY, 1985).
Helen Benedict, "Demons, goblins, and autobiography," *San Francisco Review of Books*, September 1978.
Helen Benedict, *Portraits in Print: A collection of profiles and the stories behind them* (New York, 1991).
Lisa Jones, *The Isaac Bashevis Singer Archive* (Austin, Texas, 1996)

NELSON MANDELA (P. 87)
Nelson Mandela, *The long walk to freedom* (Boston, 1994).

KIM DAE-JUNG (P. 89)
Kim Dae-jung, *Brev från fängelset* (Stockholm, 1999).

MAX PERUTZ (P. 93)
Communiqué from Anders Lundgren written for this exhibition project.
Max Perutz, *I wish I'd made you angry earlier* (Cold Spring Harbor, 1998).

ROGER SPERRY (P. 97)
Roger Sperry, "The great cerebral commissure," *Scientific American*, January, 1964.
"Special issue in honor of Roger W. Sperry," *Neuropsychologia* 36 (1998), 953-1076.
Norman H. Horowitz, "Roger Wolcott Sperry," http://www.nobel.se/medicine/articles/sperry/index.html.

FRIDTJOF NANSEN (P. 101)
Irwin Abrams, *The Nobel Peace Prize and the Laureates: An Illustrated Biographical History, 1901–1987* (Boston, 1998).

AUGUST KROGH (P. 103)
Communiqué from Jan Lindsten written for this exhibition project.
Bodil Schmidt-Nielsen, *August & Marie Krogh: Lives in Science* (Oxford, 1995).

RICHARD FEYNMAN (P. 105)
Communiqué from Anders Bárány written for this exhibition project.
Richard Feynman, *Surely You're Joking, Mr. Feynman!* (New York, 1985).

RABINDRANATH TAGORE (P. 107)
Communiqué from Stephen Farran-Lee written for this exhibition project.
Krishna Dutta & Andrew Robinson, *Rabindranath Tagore: The Myriad-Minded Man* (1995).
Amartya Sen, "Tagore and his India," *The New York Review*, June 26, 1997, 55–63.

SELMA LAGERLÖF (P. 111)
Communiqué from Stephen Farran-Lee written for this exhibition project.
Selma Lagerlöf, *En saga om en saga och andra sagor* (Stockholm, 1908).

CHARLES TOWNES (P. 113)
Communiqué from Sven Widmalm written for this exhibition project.

LINUS PAULING (P. 115)
Communiqué from Anders Lundgren written for this exhibition project.
http://www.paulingexhibit.org/exhibit/body_process.html

ERWIN SCHRÖDINGER (P. 119)
Communiqué from Anders Bárány written for this exhibition project.

HENRY DUNANT (P. 121)
Irwin Abrams, *The Nobel Peace Prize and the Laureates: An Illustrated Biographical History, 1901–1987* (Boston, 1998).

ALEXANDER FLEMING (P. 123)
Communiqué from Monika Starendal written for this exhibition project.

WILHELM RÖNTGEN (P. 125)
Bettyann Holtzmann Kevles, *Naked to the bone: Medical imaging in the twentieth century* (New Brunswick, NJ, 1997).

PEYTON ROUS (P. 127)
Communiqué from Monika Starendal written for this exhibition project.
Carol L. Moberg, "Peyton Rous: American physician and pathologist," in *Notable twentieth-century scientists*, ed. Emily J. McMurray (New York, 1995).
Carol L. Moberg, "Peyton Rous, inquiring naturalist: Cancer and the sarcoma virus," *Search*, March 1991, 9.

IRÈNE JOLIOT-CURIE AND FRÉDÉRIC JOLIOT (P. 131)
Communiqué from Anders Lundgren written for this exhibition project.

JOSEPH BRODSKY (P. 133)
Communiqué from Nina Burton written for this exhibition project.
Joseph Brodsky, Nobel lecture in *Les Prix Nobel* 1987.
Of thoughts and words: the relation between language and mind, proceedings of Nobel Symposium 92, Stockholm, Sweden, August, 8–12, 1994 (London, 1995), ed. Sture Allén.

JANE ADDAMS (P. 135)
Irwin Abrams, *The Nobel Peace Prize and the Laureates: An Illustrated Biographical History, 1901–1987* (Boston, 1998).

C.T.R. WILSON (P. 137)
Communiqué from Sven Widmalm written for this exhibition project.

ARNE TISELIUS (P. 139)
Communiqué from Anders Lundgren written for this exhibition project.

MARTIN LUTHER KING, JR. (P. 141)
Irwin Abrams, *The Nobel Peace Prize and the Laureates: An Illustrated Biographical History, 1901–1987* (Boston, 1998).
Martin Luther King, Jr., *I Have a Dream: Writings and speeches that changed the world,* ed. James M. Washington (New York, 1992).
Martin Luther King, Jr, Nobel lecture in *Les Prix Nobel* 1964.

SANTIAGO RAMÓN Y CAJAL (P. 143)
Communiqué from Jan Lindsten written for this exhibition project.
Santiago Ramón y Cajal, *Recollections of my life* (1901–1917; Cambridge, MA, 1989).
Marina Bentivoglio, "Life and discoveries of Santiago Ramón y Cajal," http://www.nobel.se/medicine/articles/cajal/index.html

WOLE SOYINKA (P. 147)
Communiqué from Nina Burton written for this exhibition project.
Wole Soyinka, *Early Poems* (New York, 1988).
http://globetrotter.berkeley.edu/Elberg/Soyinka/soyinka-con2.html#writing

WILLIAM BUTLER YEATS (P. 151)
Communiqué from Stephen Farran-Lee written for this exhibition project.

GEORGE DE HEVESY (P. 153)
Communiqué from Anders Lundgren written for this exhibition project.

PIOTR KAPITSA (P. 157)
Communiqué from Anders Bárány written for this exhibition project.
Peter Kapitsa on life and science, ed. Albert Parry (New York, 1968).

FRANCIS CRICK AND JAMES D. WATSON (P. 159)
Communiqué from Monika Starendal written for this exhibition project.

CREATIVE MILIEUS (P. 163)
Communiqué from Gunnar Törnqvist written for this exhibition project.

SANTINIKETAN (P. 165)
Communiqué from Marika Hedin written for this exhibition project.

BUDAPEST (P. 167)
Katalin Papp, "Hungarian schools: Past, present and future," *Fizikai Szemle* 49 (1995), no. 5, 220–224.

COPENHAGEN (PP. 169–171)
Communiqué from Joanna Rose written for this exhibition project.
Abraham Pais, *Niels Bohr's times: in physics, philosophy, and polity* (Oxford, 1991).

COLD SPRING HARBOR (PP. 173–175)
Communiqué from Joanna Rose written for this exhibition project.
Horace Freeland Judson, *The Eighth Day of Creation: Makers of the Revolution in Biology* (1979; expanded edition Cold Spring Harbor, 1996).

BASEL INSTITUTE FOR IMMUNOLOGY (PP. 177–179)
25 years BII: Anniversary publication (Basel, 1996).
Ulrika Björkstén, "Anarki och kaos skapar nobelpristagare," *Ny Teknik* 1997, nr 42.
Thomas Söderqvist, *Hvilken kamp for at undslippe: En biografi om immunologen og nobelpristagaren Niels Kaj Jerne* (Valby, 1998).

THE PASTEUR INSTITUTE (PP. 181–183)
François Jacob, *The statue within* (1987; Cold Spring Harbor, 1995).
François Jacob, The Pasteur Institute, http://www.nobel.se/medicine/articles/jacob/index.html.

CERN (PP. 185–186)
Communiqué from Sven Widmalm written for this exhibition project.

THE CHICAGO SCHOOL OF ECONOMICS (P. 189)
Lives of the Laureates: Thirteen Nobel Economists, eds. William Breit & Roger W. Spencer (Cambridge, MA, 1995).
http://cepa.newschool.edu/het/schools/chicago.htm

BERKELEY (PP. 191–192)

John L. Heilbron & Robert W. Seidel,
*Lawrence and his laboratory: a history of the
Lawrence Berkeley Laboratory* (Berkeley,
1989).

Ahmed Zewail, autobigraphy in *Les Prix
Nobel 1999* (Stockholm 2000).

CAMBRIDGE (PP. 195–197)

Communiqué from Marika Hedin written
for this exhibition project.

Peter Kapitsa on life and science, ed. Albert
Parry (New York, 1968).

Max Perutz, *I wish I'd made you angry earlier*
(Cold Spring Harbor, 1998)

PARIS (PP. 201–203)

Communiqué from Magnus Jacobsson
written for this exhibition project.

Sylvia Beach, *Shakespeare and Company, the
story of an American Bookshop in Paris* (New
York, 1959).

Ernest Hemingway, *A Moveable Feast* (New
York, 1964).

TOKYO (P. 205)

Communiqué from Stephen Farran-Lee
written for this exhibition project.

VIENNA (PP. 207–208)

Communiqué from Gunnar Törnqvist
written for this exhibition project.

THE SOLVAY CONFERENCES (P. 211)

Communiqué from Anders Bárány written
for this exhibition project.

THE ICBL (P. 213)

Jody Williams, "The International
Campaign to Ban Landmines—A Model
for Disarmament Initiatives?" http://
www.nobel.se/peace/articles/williams/
index.html.

Credits for pictures and artifacts

p. 10. Photo by Jan Eve Olsson.

p. 12. Gao Xingjian.

p. 13. AIP, Emilio Segrè Visual Archives.

p. 14–17. The Nobel Foundation.

p. 18. The Nobel Foundation. Photo by Reklamfotograferna, Borlänge.

p. 19. The Nobel Foundation.

p. 20. Top: The Nobel Foundation. Below: Nobelmuseet i Karlskoga. Photo by Gabriel Hildebrand.

p. 21 Nobelmuseet i Karlskoga. Photo by Gabriel Hildebrand.

p. 22 Left: Photo by Gabriel Hildebrand. Right: The Nobel Foundation. Photo by Jan Eve Olsson.

p. 23. Top: Photo by Gabriel Hildebrand. Bottom: The Nobel Foundation.

p. 24. Photo by Jan Eve Olsson.

p. 25. Left: Photo by Jan Eve Olsson. Right: Nobelmuseet i Karlskoga. Photo by Jan Eve Olsson.

p. 26. Knudsens fotosenter, Oslo.

p. 27. Pressens bild, Stockholm.

p. 28. The Nobel Foundation.

p. 29. The Nobel Foundation. Photo by Gabriel Hildebrand.

p. 30. Photo by Gabriel Hildebrand.

p. 31. Kungl. Myntkabinettet. Photo by Jan Eve Olsson.

p. 32. Top: The Nobel Foundation. Below: Pressens bild, Stockholm.

p. 33. Top: The Nobel Foundation. Below: Pressens bild, Stockholm.

p. 34. Left: Royal Library, Stockholm.

p. 35. Left: AIP, Emilio Segrè Visual Archives.

p. 37. Princeton University Library.

p. 38. National Portrait Gallery, London.

p. 40. Musée Curie, Paris. Photo by Gabriel Hildebrand.

p. 41–42. ACJC – Archives Curie et Joliot-Curie, Paris.

p. 43. Musée Curie, Paris. Photo by Gabriel Hildebrand.

p. 44. Roger-Viollet, Paris.

p. 45. Eoin O'Brien, Dublin.

p. 46. Photo by Jan Eve Olsson

p. 47. Pressens Bild, Stockholm.

p. 48. Satya Sain.

p. 49. Tom Bonnalt, Stockholm.

p. 50. Photo by Jan Eve Olsson

p. 51–53. Jevgenij Borisovitj Pasternak.

p. 54. Linda Pauling Kamb. Photo by Gabriel Hildebrand.

p. 55. Linda Pauling Kamb.

p. 56. Associated Press. Ava Helen and Linus Pauling Papers, Oregon State University, Corvallis, Oregon.

p. 55. Linda Pauling Kamb.

p. 58–59. Ahmed Zewail.

p. 60–61. Wolf-Georg Forssmann.

p. 62. Cold Spring Harbor Laboratory. Photo by Jan Eve Olsson.

p. 63. Cold Spring Harbor Laboratory Archives.

p. 64. Top: Cold Spring Harbor Laboratory Archives. Below: American Philosophical Society, Philadelphia.

p. 65. American Philosophical Society, Philadelphia.

p. 66. Catharina Engström. Photo by Gabriel Hildebrand.

p. 67. Kungliga Biblioteket, Stockholm.

p. 68–69. Pressens bild.

p. 70. The Mainichi Newspapers.

p. 71. The Museum of Japanese Modern Literature.

p. 72. United Nations. Kungliga Biblioteket, Stockholm.

p. 73. United Nations.

p. 74. Top: Svenska Turistföreningen. Photo by Gabriel Hildebrand. Below: Kungliga Biblioteket, Stockholm.

p. 75. Top and bottom: United Nations. Middle: Hammarskjöldbiblioteket, Uppsala.

p. 76–77. Yukawa Institute for Theoretical Physics, Kyoto University.

p. 78. Left (top and bottom): Yukawa Institute for Theoretical Physics, Kyoto University. Right (top and bottom): Mrs Sumi Yukawa. Photo by Gabriel Hildebrand.

p. 79. Mrs. Sumi Yukawa. Photo by Gabriel Hildebrand.

p. 80. Harry Ransom Humanities Research Center, Austin, Texas.

p. 81. Princeton University Library.

p. 82. Harry Ransom Humanities Research Center, Austin, Texas.

p. 83–84. Congrat-Butler. Harry Ransom Humanities Research Center, Austin, Texas.

p. 85. Sylvia Ary. Harry Ransom Humanities Research Center, Austin, Texas.

p. 86. Bull's Press, Stockholm.

p. 87. Pressens bild, Stockholm.

p. 88–91. Kim Dae-Jung. Artifact photos by Gabriel Hildebrand.

p. 92. Max Perutz, Medical Research Council, Cambridge. Photo by Jan Eve Olsson.

p. 93. Max Perutz.

p. 94. Max Perutz, Medical Research Council, Cambridge. Photo below by Gabriel Hildebrand.

p. 95. Top: Photo by Gabriel Hildebrand. Below: Max Perutz, Medical Research Council, Cambridge.

p. 96. Norma Sperry. Photo by Jan Eve Olsson.

p. 97. Norma Sperry.

p. 98. Norma Sperry. Photo by Jan Eve Olsson.

p. 99. Oberlin College. Photo by Gabriel Hildebrand.

p. 100–101. Nasjonalbiblioteket avdeling Oslo, Billedsamlingen.

p. 102. Top: Medicinhistorisk museum, Copenhagen. Photo by Jan Eve Olsson. Below: Det Kongelige Bibliotek, Copenhagen.

p. 103. Det Kongelige Bibliotek, Copenhagen.

p. 104. California Institute of Technology Archives. Top right: Photo by Jan Eve Olsson.

p. 105. Tom Harvey/California Institute of Technology.

p. 106. Visva-Bharati, Santiniketan.

p. 107. Photo by Jan Eve Olsson.

p. 108–109. Visva-Bharati, Santiniketan.

p. 110. Mårbacka. Photo by Jan Eve Olsson.

p. 111. Mårbacka.

p. 112. AIP Meggers Gallery of Nobel Laureates.

p. 113. AIP, Emilio Segrè Visual Archives.

p. 114. Top: Linda Pauling Kamb. Photo by Gabriel Hildebrand; Below: Ava Helen and Linus Pauling Papers, Oregon State University, Corvallis, Oregon. Photo by Jan Eve Olsson.

p. 115. Ava Helen and Linus Pauling Papers, Oregon State University, Corvallis, Oregon.

p. 116. United Press. Ava Helen and Linus Pauling Papers, Oregon State University, Corvallis, Oregon.

p. 117. Linda Pauling Kamb. Photo by Jan Eve Olsson.

p. 118–119. Photos: Ruth Braunizer. Notebook: Zentralbibliothek für Physik in Wien.

p. 120. Top: Museo Nazionale del Risorgimento Italiano, Torino. Below: Musée International de la Croix-Rouge et du Croissant-Rouge. Photo by Jan Eve Olsson.

p. 121. The Nobel Foundation.

p. 122–123. Alexander Fleming Laboratory Museum (St Mary's NHS Trust, London).

p. 124–125. Deutsches Museum, Munich.

p. 126: American Philosophical Society, Philadelphia.

p. 127: Rockefeller Archive Center, Sleepy Hollow, New York.

p. 128: Rockefeller University, New York. Photo by Jan Eve Olsson.

p. 127: Rockefeller Archive Center, Sleepy Hollow, New York.

p. 130–131. ACJC – Archives Curie et Joliot-Curie, Paris.

p. 132. Bengt Jangfeldt, Stockholm.

p. 133. Mikhail Miltchik, St. Petersburg.

p. 134. Top left: Jane Addams Memorial Collection, University Library, The University of Illinois at Chicago. Top right and below: Swarthmore College Peace Collection, Swarthmore, PA.

p. 135. Swarthmore College Peace Collection, Swarthmore, PA.

p. 136. Royal Society, London.

p. 137. Nobel Foundation.

p. 138. Medicinhistoriska museet, Uppsala. Photo by Jan Eve Olsson.

p. 139. Carolina Rediviva, Uppsala.

p. 140. B. Fitch/Black Star Photos.

p. 141. Pressens bild.

p. 142–145. Museo Cajal, Madrid.

p. 146. Wole Soyinka. Photos by Jan Eve Olsson.

p. 147–149. Wole Soyinka.

p. 150. National Gallery of Ireland, Dublin.

p. 151. Photo by Gabriel Hildebrand.

p. 152. Niels Bohr Arkivet, Copenhagen. Photo by Jan Eve Olsson.

p. 153–154. Niels Bohr Arkivet, Copenhagen.

p. 155. Top. Niels Bohr Arkivet, Copenhagen. Photo by Jan Eve Olsson. Below. Ingrid de Hevesy.

p. 156. Top: Photo by Gabriel Hildebrand. Below: AIP, Emilio Segrè Visual Archives, Margrethe Bohr Collection.

p. 157. Cavendish Laboratory, Cambridge.

p. 158. Cold Spring Harbor Laboratory Archives.

p. 159. Science Photo Library.

p. 161. Leonard McCombe/Timepix.

p. 162. Motesiczky Charitable Trust

p. 164. Top: Visva-Bharati, Santiniketan. Below: Marika Hedin.

p. 165. Visva-Bharati, Santiniketan.

p. 166. Top and bottom right: Niels Bohr Arkivet, Copenhagen.

p. 167. Pressens bild.

p. 168–171. Niels Bohr Arkivet, Copenhagen.

p. 172–175. Cold Spring Harbor Laboratory Archives.

p. 176–179. Basel Institute for Immunology.

p. 180–183. Institut Pasteur/François Jacob.

p. 184. CERN. Below: Photo by Gabriel Hildebrand.

p. 186. CERN. Top left: Photo by Gabriel Hildebrand.

p. 187. CERN. Top: Photo by Gabriel Hildebrand.

p. 188–189. The Nobel Foundation.

p. 190–193. Lawrence Berkeley National Laboratory.

p. 194. Top: Photo by Jan Eve Olsson.

Below: The Cambridge Studio, Cambridge.

p. 195. Cavendish Laboratory, Cambridge.

p. 196. Top left and below right: AIP, Emilio Segrè Visual Archives. Top right: Niels Bohr Arkivet, Copenhagen. Below left: Cavendish Laboratory, Cambridge.

p. 197. Left: AIP, Emilio Segrè Visual Archives. Top right: Cold Spring Harbor Laboratory Archives. Below left: Cavendish Laboratory, Cambridge.

p. 198. Top: Photo by Jan Eve Olson. Below Cavendish Laboratory, Cambridge.

p. 199. Churchill Archives Centre, Churchill College, Cambridge.

p. 200. Top: Museum voor schone kunsten, Gent. Below: Roger-Viollet, Paris.

p. 201. Photo by Jan Eve Olsson

p. 202. Top left: Princeton University Library. Top right: Harry Ransom Humanities Research Center, Austin, Texas. Below left and right: Roger-Viollet, Paris.

p. 203. Top left: Mario Dondero, Paris. Top right and below: Roger-Viollet, Paris.

p. 204. Top: Bungei Jidai. Shotaro Akiyama/The Mainichi Newspapers.

p. 205. The Museum of Japanese Modern Literature.

p. 206. Albertina, Wien.

p. 207. Carl Hanser Verlag.

p. 208. Left: Photo by Jan Eve Olsson. Right: Carl Hanser Verlag.

p. 209. Institute for the History of Medicine, Vienna.

p. 210. Institut international de physique Solvay, courtesy AIP, Emilio Segrè Visual Archives.

p. 211. AIP, Emilio Segrè Visual Archives.

p. 212. Top: Photo by Jan Eve Olsson. Below: John Rodsted.

p. 213. John Rodsted.

p. 214. Top: Tim Grant. Below: John Rodsted.

p. 215. Tim Grant.

Name Index

ACKNOWLEDGMENTS

THE INTERNATIONAL ADVISORY COMMITTEE OF THE CENTENNIAL EXHIBITION:

Paolo Galluzzi, chairman	Wolf Peter Fehlhammer	John L. Heilbron	George Steiner
James A. Bennett	Dominique Ferriot	Frederic L. Holmes	Hiroyuki Yoshikawa
Sir Neil Cossons	Bernard S. Finn	Thomas P. Hughes	Harriet Zuckerman
Umberto Eco	Robert Friedel	Simon Schaffer	

THE FOLLOWING PERSONS HAVE CONTRIBUTED TO THE CONTENT OF THE EXHIBITION:

Irwin Abrams	Sture Forsén	Anders Lundgren	Helge Skoog
Wilhelm Agrell	Tore Frängsmyr	Peter Lundqvist	Gudmund Smith
Birgitta Alani	Karl Grandin	Agneta Lundström	Monika Starendal
Sture Allén	Margaretha Hartzell	Anders Mellbourn	Anna Stenkula
Olov Amelin	Marika Hedin	Bengt Nagel	Åsa Sundelin
Anders Bárány	Magnus Jacobsson	Olav Njölstad	Olof G. Tandberg
Ulrika Björkstén	Bengt Jangfeldt	Jan Nolin	Mia Thelander
Margareta Bond-Fahlberg	Kersti Johnson	Olle Nordberg	Per Thullberg
Mats Brunander	Thomas Kaiserfeld	Eva Nordenson	Ola Thufvesson
Nina Burton	Ulla Keding Olofsson	Gunilla Nordlund	Christina Tillfors
Anna Busch	Anita Klum	Jan Prawitz	Öyvind Tönnesson
Annagreta Dyring	Ulf Larsson	Stig Ramel	Gunnar Törnqvist
Eric Dyring	Birgitta Lemmel	Joanna Rose	Sven Widmalm
Anders Ekström	Julia Lindkvist	Adam D. Rothfeld	Katarina Villner
Gunnar Eliasson	Svante Lindqvist	Ingegerd Runesson	Thomas Wright
Lena Embertsen	Jan Lindsten	Arne Ruth	Urban Wråkberg
Åke Erlandsson	Anna Ljunggren	Josefin Rönnbäck	
Kristina Fallenius	Bengt Lundberg	Francis Sejersted	
Stephen Farran-Lee	Geir Lundestad	Fredrik Skog	

EXHIBITION PRODUCTION

Curator: Olov Amelin
Design: Björn Ed, designer; Camilla Ed, stage designer; Gyllenpalm & Sohlman Arkitekter AB, architects.
Film production: Suecia Film AB: Anders Wahlgren; University College of Film, Radio, Television and Theatre, Stockholm: Marika Heidebäck, Fanny Josephsson, Terese Mörnvik, Kirsi Nevanti, Lisa Partby, Karin Wegsjö; Handicap International: Jean-Charles Betrancourt; Christian Peters; Motion Dynamic, Per Wickander.
Graphic design: Kingston AB.
Light design: Ljusdesign.
Blacksmith: Peder Wolfbrandt smide.
Carpentry: Långholmens Snickeri; Snickeri Kversus.
Harnessing: Svenska Inredningssadelmakeriet.
Models: Stig Viktorsson modeller AB.
Glass: Planglasteknik Stockholm AB.
Multimedia consultant: Jonas Lindkvist Design AB.
Sound design: Anna Tullberg, Audio Data Lab.
Refurbishment of the exhibition hall in Stockholm: Skanska, Algeba byggkonsulter AB, Q-konsult Margareta Cramér, Brandskyddslaget AB, Bostadsbolaget Elisabeth Edsjö Arkitektkontor AB, BWB Elkonsult, VVV Ingenjörer AB, Storköksbyrån i Stockholm AB.